LEADERS! OR MANAGERS?
— AND —
DISCOVER YOUR TALENTS

KELE D. GABOR

ISBN: 978-1-955403-08-5 (sc)
ISBN: 978-1-955403-09-2 (e)

Because of the dynamic nature of the Internet, any web addresses or links contained in this book may have changed since publication and may no longer be valid. The views expressed in this work are solely those of the author and do not necessarily reflect the views of the publisher, and the publisher hereby disclaims any responsibility for them.

CONTENTS

ADDENDUM

PROLOGUE

This book is written for every voting-age person to read, but this Prologue is mainly addressed to the retirees!

Getting to an old age is a blessing in spite of the aching joints when the golden times turn to rusty years. Living long in some discomfort is better than dying young. Also, the longer one lives the more opportunity one has to learn and to gain more experience. The more one experiences the wiser one gets, of course with certain inherent limitations. These limitations include one's capacity to learn, the range, type and the impact of one's environment, timing, age and circumstances as they were experienced, to list but a few.

There are obvious signs of aging such as more frequent visits to the doctors than the yearly checkup, and taking longer to recover from the workout than the duration of the exercise. And if you're over 80 your sense of well-being is replaced by symptoms and after you give up all your bad habits you don't notice any improvements. You can fill in your own unique signs of aging in your diary at your pleasure, but I don't think anybody will be interested.

When you think you have retired and made it you may be moving into a convenient rut and going downhill.

Old folks cheer up! All human knowledge is based on experiences! So, saying, "The older you are the wiser you are." is true! So get up out of your chair, start teaching, sharing knowledge while learning from experiences you discovered the hard way to the younger generations so they won't make the same mistakes. If you are still undecided take a small step forward, write your experiences down, share them and later publish them. Teach new skills, open eyes and minds to new ideas, and educate. Many old people are sitting in a rocking chair just because it moves, but it doesn't get you anywhere! The rest of your life may be too short to be wasted.

Brains of older people are slower because they know so much. People might not decline mentally with age, it just takes them longer to recall facts because they have more information in their brains. According to Dr. Michael Ramscar, the human brain works slower in old age because we store more information over time. It is like your computer when the hard drive gets full it takes longer to access information.

Some older people go upstairs to another room to get something but when they get there, they forget what they came for. It might not be a memory problem, it might be nature's way of telling you, "Need more exercise". - Instead of taking "Prevagen", it'll be cheaper to delete some of the unneeded information from your hard drive.

Don't forget, you have a lot of *answers* but the problem is that nobody is *asking*, so tell them anyway. If some of you could sell your valuable experiences many of you could be millionaires!

Life ends when you stop dreaming, hope ends when you stop believing, love ends when you stop caring; and, friendship ends when you stop sharing.

In this spirit I would like to share some of my experiences and acquired knowledge, Venture Capitalists would be delighted to know about or could benefit from, with many parents, teachers, voters, decision makers, leaders and managers. Or perhaps, this book might clarify situations you cannot yet explain. Some of these experiences and observations may not yet have much empirical data to support or prove. Some may also be politically incorrect. Nevertheless, it is well worth more than just mere consideration. Possibly, you might be the one who will prove or disprove my unverified claims.

Best solutions to problems might not be new brilliant ideas, but sometimes by making old and proven methods work!

To be continued in the EPILOGUE!

INTRODUCTION

I grew up during WWII in Central Europe with frequent exposure to air raids, hunger, shootings, and physical conflicts. I lived under occupation by foreign armies, and dug up unexploded landmines in return for warm soup. I was put in political prison, interrogated by the communist secret police and lived under many forms of governments. All of these left me with a lot of unwanted memories and experiences. Yet, in retrospect, they were helpful to put things in different perspectives as they opened my eyes and mind to look beyond the obvious and visible, and also to learn from bad experiences.

- I believe more wisdom comes from living than just reading and studying.

For example, during occupations by different countries and armies I noticed some common denominators besides robbing us blind, taking everything of value including all our weapons and leaving us totally defenseless. With each newly created government, most of them served the often changing occupiers, put the previous leaders in prison, sent them to a Gulag, Concentration or Work camp, or simply eliminated them. Nevertheless, they all went far beyond these steps, the new rulers also penalized their families including their children. Examples: many of the children were also sent to forced labor camps. Any of them showing resistance ended up in uranium or coal mines, or much worse. All were denied regular education. When the boys became 20 they were inducted into the military but instead of military training they were permanently assigned to work duty. Those sons and daughters who didn't have to suffer the same disastrous fate as their fathers or mothers were simply kicked out of schools, colleges, or universities, just like I was.

It is beyond description and comprehension how evil and inhuman ways some of the unwanted families were dealt with. I'm afraid to describe here any of the gory details of these terrible events which had taken place with some regularity.[1]

Historically this terrible treatment of ruling families and their offspring, like kings, tsars and emperors could be explained as any one of the surviving offspring of the family or close relatives could make a legal claim to the throne at any time. However, in my experience there were no royal families involved, just very respected individuals in high positions either in government or in private industries: those who were perceived as possible threats to the new regime because of their popularity. Just as Stalin dealt with some of his best generals after the war was over, by eliminating the most popular ones. - His paranoia in action.

The above mentioned common behavior by oppressive governments puzzled me for many years until I joined the ROTC (Reserve Officer Training Corp), served in the military and also worked for a long time in the private industry that included large, medium, small and start-up companies. During these times I noticed that every good and natural leader I encountered and learned to respect

---

[1] My family experiences and a few others are presented in the Appendix.

had a mother or father in high position. Or at least a grandparent as inheriting certain abilities might skip a generation or two[2].

Coincidence?

I'm sure there are exceptions but if it isn't a coincidence, it could be the reason why unwanted leaders' children are also suppressed, penalized or killed by the oppressive new regime in power.

Maybe, our education and training place too much emphasis on the environmental factors and not enough on the genetic side.

(Did you ever wonder why some ranchers pay so much money for the services of certain bulls to hopefully pass on some of the desired traits to produce better breeds? Just look at the race-horses, where the price is much higher, sometimes hundreds of thousands dollars for breeding to improve performance or just to pass on the desired genes. Stud service to improve breeds in physical appearance, abilities and temperaments is in practice for most domesticated animals around the world.)

My experiences, my findings, inferences and views I have drawn from actual events are presented in the following chapters.

---

[2] Scientific term is "atavism".

LEADERSHIP

I distinguish between naturally good leaders and leadership attained by appointments, votes, force, promotions or political means. I'll explain the many differences later.

Initially, I attributed my good fortune of frequent promotions to the fact that I was a believer in and an avid user of the Franklin Reality Model (FRM), valued people, time and practiced Dr. W. Edwards Deming's theory for managing companies. Of course, all my success was directly related to people with whom I worked, being either hired by me or inherited from the previous manager, director, or VP. I had good luck picking my direct reports[3], but it might be more than just luck so I will explain my hiring methods later.

Basically, the FRM model explains what the main motivators are to bring individuals to action. But for me it was much more since I used this model to find out about myself and to understand the underlying reasons for some of my past and recent actions as to why I acted as I did.

When having these reflections, one finds out a lot about oneself and I became quite proficient at applying it to my direct reports and other individuals. This is how I came to know what is

---

[3] People directly reporting to me.

important to each individual and what are the main motivating factors to cause them to do things better or spur them to action. As a result of treating all my employees fairly and applying the required motivational factors tailored to at least the lead people, my teams were always productive. This is very important in our highly competitive world.

You can get people to do what you want by understanding them.

Some of my direct reports valued time off, the others praise, others title and recognition, etc. Understanding these factors gave me some additional tools to encourage them to be more productive, since I have always believed in rewarding good behavior, quality work and productivity in a way the person would truly appreciate it. So, giving credit where credit is due and showing your thanks for a job well done, the way the individual would appreciate it the most. They're deserving of this, and you owe it to them.

Here I must mention *politics* and *diplomacy* as some consider using the FRM model for others' advantage is playing politics or manipulating people. However, using the FRM by anybody is more like playing *diplomacy* or making a *deal* where both parties benefit. Politics is a necessary evil and it is played, to some extent, in almost every situation and organization. You can ignore political events, but they won't ignore *you*! More eloquently said by Pericles in 430 B.C. "Just because you don't take interest in politics doesn't mean politics won't take an interest in you."

In my view, people who take an interest in politics, understand the issues and are knowledgeable about the candidates when voting, care more about the future of the nation and the next generation than those who don't.

Politics can be mean and downright evil or can be more like diplomacy. I prefer the latter. Nowadays, dirty politics seems to be the norm where one side openly attacks the other instead of working together for the benefit of the people, even though the elected officials took an oath to serve them. Few would disagree with Edward Langley's comment, "What this country needs are more unemployed politicians."

Even before learning about Management Science I could often recognize an individual's potential and easily distinguish between manager and leader types. Peter's *Principle*[4] applies to us all as we all have some limitations, including me. Differences among people with titles vary but true leader types are quite different from managers, who usually fade out in their respective positions much sooner. They are more concerned about the near future than the long term and often do things for their own benefit instead of others. In every higher position the operating time and the value of it increases as the level of responsibility grows. While a supervisor must think weeks ahead, a manager must extend it to at least a year. Directors usually work five years ahead while CEOs (Chief Executive Officer) and Presidents must think in an even longer term. So, the biggest difference between employees and the upper echelon is the timeframe in which they work and operate. Being in a higher position does not make them smarter than anyone else below, but the pressure and responsibilities increase with each promotion. In fact, I consider the *contributors* to be the smartest people. They have more time for: their families, extracurricular activities, self and technical improvement, quality time, and fun times while their roles are just as important and on occasion, more so than anyone else's above them.

---

[4] L. J. Peter's observation was that people in a hierarchy tend to rise to their "level of incompetence".

Individuals with natural leadership talents and abilities can be observed even at an early age when children in group settings gather around a classmate in recess who initiates activities with multiple followers doing or wanting to do similar things, or just wanting to participate in some capacity. On one occasion I noticed leadership abilities in a 2-year old when he was playing with his older siblings and cousins. To my surprise, he was the one who initiated or was asked for new games or activities. This happened among the other five children during an entire weekend and he was happy to play the role.

During my career I noticed that while the follower types could be trained to become excellent military officers (up to the ranks of field officers[5]), managers (up to directors) in the industry, or as congressmen or senators in politics. But it is mainly the natural leader type that gets to the top, the exceptions being a political appointee, nepotism, voted in by the general public, or where money, force or repaying a favor is involved.

I have attended or lectured in many management and leadership classes and have found all attendees exceptionally bright, however, some of them could never become leaders as they didn't understand or didn't appreciate the importance of time management, fair and equal treatment of all employees, or they failed to recognize the importance of the positive *shared vision* for the future. Some of the class participants would even argue for delaying decisions until all facts became known. It seemed like some who had leadership abilities could be trained, but for those who didn't have those abilities no training could make them a true leader.

---

[5]   Field officers rank goes up to Lieutenant Colonel.

Unfortunately, the abilities in leadership are often ignored in politics as neither many of the voters nor the media can recognize people who have leadership talents or are not able to distinguish between empty promises and the truth during debates. Instead, the average person tends to vote for their party candidates, whoever promises the most, or based on looks and *symmetry index*[6] of the candidates.

It has been shown that people with good looks and a high symmetry index of their faces are much more likely to win over the ones without good looks and less attractive features, this is so, regardless of their differing qualifications. The same bias applies in promoting individuals when it comes to height - the taller ones are more likely to be promoted.

Imagine that if the best qualified leader for your district, county, state or country who is badly needed to improve conditions or save a nation is missing an arm, is bald, fat, has an unpleasing voice, or stutters, is short in stature, is rough in mannerisms or has an asymmetric face, that candidate would never be voted in by the general public.

One of the best and most successful Roman Emperors, Tiberius Claudius could never be elected by the American voters because of an unattractive appearance, his stutter, clumsiness in manner, combined with his use of unique methods to solve problems. On the other hand, American voters would have no problem electing a handsome orator like baneful Caligula.

---

[6] Measured by comparing the differences of the two sides of the face. Higher the index the more attractive is the person, i.e. even a doe prefers to mate with a buck with symmetrical antlers.

In our Representative Republic we deserve the Government we elected and if it becomes dysfunctional or stops serving its citizens, we obviously sent the wrong Representatives to Congress. Therefore, I wish there were a program to convince voters *not* to vote unless they understand the issues, know the facts and the candidates.

GOOD LEADERSHIP

There are hundreds of books published on leadership but I only read a few as I wanted to develop my own theories and definitions based on my personal experiences. Before I list the most important attributes, according to my research, of a *"true leader"*, I need to mention the critical prerequisites for a good leader I found by augmenting the FRM (Franklin Reality Model).

According to many scholars, authors, and experts in Management Science many attributes are required for being a true leader and especially a top notch *"good leader"*. To mention a few attributes I found in these books: good communication skills, ability to motivate people, good orator, have charisma, the ability to sell their talents and qualifications whether it is true or false to the followers, keeping promises, setting an example with professional behavior, a high symmetry index, strong views with which employees or voters identify, proposing meaningful solutions to nagging problems and have power by votes, titles or promotion (money, military, force or fear).

My take is simpler, as leaders I respect have a positive and inspirational *Vision* for the future which the followers not only buy into but often enthusiastically support, *integrity* demonstrated by being true to promises, and doing the tasks with commitment to benefitting the employees, the company, the community, the country and of course, the customers: in doing it all for the *benefits of others.*

Good leaders look ahead, guided by their *vision*, and don't depend on popularity as they must make decisions for the *future*, while the average person mainly considers the present. Some actions by the *leaders* may be very unpopular, but could prove to be the best strategy to preserve a nation. Therefore, overly popular presidents, in my mind, are often doing worse than a questionable job for the future of any country! Typically, the popular presidents' decision making process is primarily focused on pleasing the public, which is like driving ahead based on what one sees in the rearview mirror. Therefore, a *popular* President and *good leadership* is a contradiction! Popularity of songs, dance, fashion, sports figures, actors, beauty queens, or anything and anybody is a fleeting thing that changes often and comes in waves. Popularity of politicians is based on what free stuff is offered or promised to the public. Only history will have judged the abilities and performance of a national leader based on the beneficial effects for the country and its people in the long term. However, even some of the historians may confuse *leadership* with *conquerors*. Currently, the top 5 "leaders" named in history are all conquerors, based on how large they built their empires. The list starts with Alexander the Great and ends with the largest empire builder, Genghis Khan. I contend that; *Good leadership should be judged on how one protects the people, the nation, and how conducive an environment was provided to benefit its people by ways of prospering and growth, and not the least how Nature is treated and how its young people are prepared to lead and love the world.*

A popularity index just shows what the leader is doing for the people right *now* and has no predictive *value* of one's true leadership talents and abilities! In my mind, when the voting public consistently favors the President is around 50% or more, this can portend disasters for the country. Therefore, I sometimes wonder how popular some of the great leaders in their time in American history were, for example President Lincoln. I suspect Lincoln's popularity was much lower than most of the contemporary U.S. presidents as he had the courage to make many unpopular decisions to save the nation.

In the case of politicians, the same approach to determine their leadership abilities might not apply as many congressmen may *not* be the leader types anyways. As written by an ex Senator, "Most leading politicians are more interested in power and money than fairness and justice."

Ambitious and power hungry individuals often fight for control, but they fail to be good leaders. In politics, I have very seldom seen a good leader elected by the voters as many people cannot distinguish between charisma or good looks and leadership talents and abilities.

Many people are easily misled, often voting with their feelings and ignoring facts and figures or going by what their favorite biased news reporters say. The now-generation seems to put more focus on what the candidates say and don't say, and how the new candidate speaks, instead of what the candidate does or his accomplishments. - Actions speak louder than words.

Luckily, CEOs (Chief Executive Officers) are not placed in leadership positions by employee votes, just imagine if they were elected and the resulting dire consequences. For example; employees most likely would vote for an individual with whom they can identify. That person might not have the necessary skills in negotiating, leading, or have a *vision* which can truly be shared and inspiring, might not have the necessary connections with sales, customers, and marketing, also might not understand the required duties of a CEO, finance, economics, and the customers. However, this is not true in the military as I had seen the *right* person selected to *lead* by the fellow soldiers after the Captain was shot and the Sargent was injured. This type of picking the right leaders in combat situations has been proven by many documented events. - Maybe we should be voting like our lives depend on it.

I would love to give real examples of many "popular" presidents voted into office without any leadership qualities or skills but some people might be offended if they think or feel otherwise, or liked him and found the person attractive in spite of his shortcomings, or cannot distinguish between Leaders and Managers/Politicians.

I met and knew many CEOs and there are serious misconceptions by the public about their role, functions, qualifications, and their worth. Even the general perception of the public of the type of characters they are is typically wrong. Many people believe they make too much money and they are dubious characters at best, thanks to mostly the entertainment industries, inexperienced professors' teachings who live in ivory towers together with biased news reporters and politicians.

I have not seen a single Hollywood film which described an honest, fair and good person in the role of a CEO. A good example is the beautiful epic film; AVATAR I, where the storyline parallels the plight of the American Indians. But instead of blaming the evil doings on the actual greedy political power and land grabbers, like the Jacksonian Democrats who started the Indian Wars and eliminated most of them, they changed the storyline and accused the greedy company and its executives of putting profit ahead of the natives' lives and lands.

"It takes one to know one."

In general the last people who could identify with good leadership might be the actors as their lives are *following* scripts and instructions from the directors to play somebody else's character. It is almost impossible for most of the actors to distinguish between *leader* and *manager* types. Those who recognize true leadership qualities and talents usually end up also as authors or directors of subsequent films or plays.

A similar scenario applies to reporters, editors and comedians as they must be preoccupied with recent past and present events and have no training to apply these happenings, incidents or actions to project their effect for the long term, and sometimes not even to the near future. Unfortunately, most people get their information from the above mentioned groups: Media, News Papers, Entertainers, and Reporters.

Contrary to popular belief, the great majority of the CEOs are fair, well meaning, honest, smart, good people who are looking out for the interests of customers, employees, the company, the stakeholders, investors, shareholders and answer to the Board of Directors. Besides the great pressure and responsibilities, the CEOs of public corporations must report and answer to more groups of people than any other position in industry or in government.

CEOs work very hard, have a lot of responsibilities, pressure and their tenure is usually short. Therefore, they need the "*golden parachute*"[7] to tide them over in case of early departure. Burn-outs, falling stock prices, economic downturns, missing commitments in delivering quality products or services, not making enough profit or going into the red, hiring the wrong people, conflict between the board of directors and the president are some of the reasons for premature departure or replacement of the CEOs.

My golden parachute never materialized because the company was bought out from another state. Therefore, they were not obligated to honor the original agreement. Out of courtesy they paid me less than 10% of the earlier agreed upon amount.

In short, as Ayn Rand put it, "If a businessman makes a mistake, he suffers the consequences. If a bureaucrat makes a mistake you suffer the consequences."

A good example is Apple Computers where a good leader type, Steve Jobs was forced out because of the conflict with the Board of Directors. Luckily Steve came back after the conflict was resolved. Steve was a real leader, although many of his direct reports called him a slave driver, but they followed him and worked a lot of extra hours because they bought into his *vision* in making Apple Co. very profitable, thereby improving and enriching the lives of customers and employees, and enhancing the company's future. Another example was at Hewlett Packard where the Board of Directors replaced the company president, but she was never given a chance to return.

Most of the complaints about the high salaries of CEOs are greed, envy, jealousy or ignorance by the critics. I know for a fact that

---

[7]   Golden parachute is a needed financial compensation in case of early departure so he/she and his/her family can survive but also used to attract good leaders for saving under-performing companies.

a bad CEO is very much an exception and a bad one could only survive in a privately owned company. Who wants to work for money and power hungry tyrants?

Many Americans make a million dollars or more but I know only one, Charles Schwab, whose yearly salary was a million dollars before WWII. When he was asked if his pay was so much because he knew so much about steel the answer was, "No," pointing out that there were many people who knew more about steel than he did. He attributed his high salary to his ability to deal with people. "I consider my ability to arouse enthusiasm among the men the greatest asset I possess."

Those who want to critique the Capitalist system, they could complain about the Monopolies, not enough competing companies but not the CEOs' salaries or their compensations. Jealousy, envy or greed is a waste of time and it is wrong whether originating from ignorance or emotion.

The New Tech-Giants are another good subject for criticism not only as Monopolies but also controlling information content followed by dissemination of their own biased views as in Google and Facebook. In fact, the entire world's social media are controlled by only 3 or 4 companies!

One could also complain about the huge banks making life difficult for the small ones.

Socialists might also criticize Capitalism because of what Winston Churchill said is true, "The inherent vice of capitalism is the unequal sharing of its blessings. The inherent blessings of Socialism is the equal sharing of its misery." - I suffered and experienced some of it. In socialism, most of the people suffer, only the top government officials enjoy power, control and comfort. Socialism can succeed for only a short time, until it runs out of productive people's money and wealth since they must take it all to prop up an inefficient government-run state. "I contend that for a nation to try to tax itself into prosperity is like a man standing in a bucket and trying to lift himself up by the handle." according to another good quote from Churchill, that I also experienced and witnessed to be true. I believe Thomas Jefferson's message, "Democracy will cease to exist when you take away from those who are willing to work and give to those who would not." gives the same warning.

We're all part of Nature where competition is the key to survival. Every living thing is either food or a host for other living things. This is nature's way to eliminate the weak and only the strong and smart can survive. This is considered the *natural selection* process. However, I prefer the more humane ways of the selection process and leaving the wild ways of nature to take their own course.

Human competition is necessary to bring the best out of people, but it comes with certain rules about fairness[8], like *respect* for all living things - whether it be human, animal or plant. Honoring other people's words, thoughts and wishes even if you disagree, don't speak about others in a bad way, and know that everyone makes mistakes and mistakes can be forgiven.

In our competitive world, where highly skilled professionals and technical workers are in demand, only honest and fair CEOs could hold onto them for the time necessary to make the company successful. This is very true in the High-Tech Start-ups. They need and depend on experienced professionals to make the company

---

[8] Currently, in sport competitions, rules unfairly permit transgenders in women's roles even though they have a definite physical strength advantage over naturally born females.

successful. No-one can do it alone, we all depend on each other and teamwork for success. Even great minds like Einstein received a lot of support, help and advice from others before he came up with the Theory of Relativity.

I'm not implying that all CEOs are angels for when dealing with competition they sometimes will resort to actions which my belief system would not allow me to do, in order to be the winner. A good example is Microsoft's Bill Gates' brilliance in outsmarting and taking advantage of competitions even though the other sides had better products for the end users. An example of Bill's success was the first IBM PC and the new MS DOS which was a single user system with limited capabilities while the competition had better platforms, faster processors and multi-user operating systems. Name recognition such as IBM was a big advantage and asset for Microsoft and helped Bill often come out on top, whether he deserved it or not.

I had three contracts with Bill and all three were late on deliveries but he was able to maintain good rapport and gain forgiveness for each failure.

I also had many positions in the high-tech industry but being a CEO was not only the most difficult and challenging but also demanded actions I was not willing to take in order to beat the competition. One could refer to my hang-up in this situation as an example of Peter's Principle catching up with me. Even after my unwanted experience as a CEO I accepted this position on a short-term basis once more.

Another example of beating the better and technologically more advanced competition was done by IBM by using their extensive financial resources. IBM simply replaced the very much more advanced and liked multiuser, multiprocessor and expensive mainframes by providing their single processor system free to Stanford University, despite objections from all the computer users and the departmental head.

Most company collapses are due to management problems but there are of course failures due to unexpected external events out of the *leadership*'s control and I will present some examples later.

It should be an easy task to identify good or bad leadership just by finding out why and how they got to the top. Was it only for power, getting rich, or to better the lives of other people? Let's see the Franklin Reality Model and the extensions and augmentation I talked about earlier.

The **Franklin Reality Model**:

4 Human Needs:	Filter A	Filter B	ACTION	BENEFITS
[To feel IMPORTANT]				
[To Love & Be loved]	[Beliefs]	[LAW]	[DO IT]	[WHO]
[To Live or Survive]}}[	]}}[	]}}}[	]}}}}}[	]
[Variety / Change] [____]	[____]	[____]	[____]	[____]
[_____]				]
[				]
[_____ Feedback Loop_____]				

Here is some basic information in order to understand the FRM and how it applies to individual action.

The four basic human needs, or one or more combinations, are motivating people to do things, providing the action is acceptable to the individual's criteria, like applying Filter A to meet the *belief* system and Filter B checks if the expected action is acceptable to the person's perception of *legality*. Examples:

1. Suppose you want to belong to a club, gang or organization to feel *important* or *to be loved* but this group requires you to do something to qualify as a member. If you think the action someone wants you to do is wrong based on your *belief* system or *illegal* by your standards, you will not do it.

2. Many times there are combinations of needs involved in bringing you to action, such as helping others may be other than just *love* as it also makes you feel good, or *important*.

3. Entrepreneurs, companies, marketing and sales are fully aware of these human needs and make sizable profits using them effectively. For example; needs for *variety* or *change* keep many companies successful and highly profitable: Fashion Designers and Industries, Travel industry, Cosmetics (operating on the highest ROI[9]), to mention a few.

4. *Love* and *be loved* are also present opportunities to be very profitable businesses as everyone wants to *love* and *be loved*. From the sex appeal industries, jewelry, hot and expensive sport cars and chocolates to flower shops.

5. Actions associated with *survival* and keeping *alive* often bypass a filter or both A and B. Even if you believe that killing wild animals or harming people is wrong, in order to save your child's life may require you to bypass your *belief* system or ignore the *law*.

The above examples should suffice to get the general idea about how the Franklin Reality Model works.

---

[9] ROI - Stands for Return On Investment.

The FEEDBACK LOOP.

My observation and experience show that not enough people use the Feedback Loop opportunity or even ask the right questions after their *actions* or *deeds*. I found that many people ignore this important phase and do not complete the FRM cycle of examining the reasons for their actions, for example, "Why did I do that?", or "What was the benefit of my action?", or "Whom did my action benefit?".

Discounting loving parents, even fewer people *plan for actions to benefit others*, yet without exception, I found these to be the best qualified, respected and natural "*good leaders*"! - *This question is my augmentation to the FRM Feedback loop and the fifth addition to the motivating factors is a positive vision for the future. Inspiring vision also brings people to action and it encompasses more than just the four top human needs!*

Therefore, my definition for *good leaders* is one who has a *shared and positive vision for the future*, high *integrity*, work to *benefit others*, and *power* in the form of title in the industry, rank in the Military, or has the majority of key votes in politics.

My conclusion of good leadership is closest to Suresh Srivastva, "Executive mind is impotent without *power, power* is dangerous without *vision*, and neither is lasting ...without the force of *integrity*."

My experiences also show that the best leaders make timely decisions, value people and time, seek others' opinions, seriously consider input from the opposition, delegate decision making to the lowest level possible and didn't have straight "A"s in schools. I attribute this to the fact that straight "A" students are more *followers* than *leaders* type as in order to get only "A"s in all subjects one has to please all their teachers and not challenge them but believe them. These pupils are unlikely to voice different opinions, rarely think for themselves, or openly disagree.

Top-notch *leaders* and *teachers* I know are fully aware, understand and truly appreciate the following:

- The Value of Time
- The Success of Perseverance
- The Pleasure of Working
- The Dignity of Simplicity
- The Worth of Character
- The Power of Kindness
- The Influence of Example
- The Obligation of Duty
- The Wisdom of Economy
- The Value of Patience
- The Improvement of Talent
- The Joy of Originating

Good leaders have causes and convictions for which they're willing to fight. Those who don't want to rock the boat are always on the sideline or left behind.

OBSERVATIONS ON USING THE FRM FEEDBACK LOOP

In High Schools, colleges, at work and in general people who use the *feedback* even on an elementary level, like only asking after their *action*, "What was the benefit for me?" avoid a lot of problems in their lives and advance much further than those who ignore this step.

For example: people using the *feedback* even on a basic level and put tattoos on their bodies or rings in their noses won't do it again. Those who try drugs or smoking will only do it once and don't get hooked. People are asking, "What was my benefit?" save themselves from a lot of trouble, don't join gangs, don't follow fashion blindly or get into bad habits. They typically educate themselves, becoming more practical, productive, and realistic about the world in which they live. They are not as much influenced by feelings, instead, usually consider the facts first. I also found these individuals to be more practical and conservatives and less liberal/progressive in their thinking. These people will take responsibility for their actions and not blame others for their own failures or shortcomings.

While tutoring the mentally gifted I asked one of my honor students why his feelings about issues seemed to be ignored, his response, " I don't ignore them as people cannot help feeling the way they do but we have a lot of options as to what to do about them."

People who ask, "What was the *benefit for others?*" (my family, school, company, community, my fellow men, the country or nation, the world) are the ones who focus on people, inspire, motivate, influence, have more talents in leadership and usually end up as good and natural leaders, if circumstances permit. They are also the ones who keep learning, improving themselves and use leadership tools more effectively in order to make a positive difference for all, at a minimum like a desired *Butterfly Effect*.[10]

I'd like to mention here an interesting event. A company CEO wanted to help unemployed people in the inner-city slums by putting in a burn-in facility close to government housing development for the newly manufactured Personal Computers. The process requires many hourly workers and minimal time for technical training. Unfortunately, he could not get the city permits for the facility and operation for several seemingly minor reasons. Later, according to a city employee; the City Mayor needed the votes of the poor to stay in power. (The poor tend to vote for those who promise the most free services. Many voters don't realize that they are being bought and made dependent on the government at the taxpayers' expense.)

This city employee went far beyond her statement and tried to prove her point with colorful charts showing that Cities, States, and Countries run by Democrats have a noticeable increase in Government assistance programs in the form of welfare checks,

---

[10] The phenomenon whereby a minute localized change in a complex system can have a large impact elsewhere.

food stamps, and free housing, and of course the resulting burden of higher taxes for the wage earners and companies. Her point was that this is the way they use taxpayer money to buy additional votes for themselves. As George Bernard Shaw put it, "A government which robs Peter to pay Paul can always depend on the support of Paul."

She even brought up the illegal migrant problems which she estimated to be over 20 million in the US at that time. She explained the situation in a rhetorical fashion by asking, "Who are the beneficiaries of the illegal emigration?" Since we didn't answer she claimed that for every 720 thousand people, regardless of their status, they get to send a representative to Washington DC. Since these illegal immigrants and their offspring tend to vote for Democrats, the party can increase its representation by 30 in the House. So open borders primarily benefit the Democratic party while putting an extra burden on US taxpayers.

- At that time I didn't take her colorful presentation to heart.

PUTTING GOOD LEADERSHIP TO WORK

Typically good leadership on all fronts are required to maintain healthy economic growth in a country and similarly to make companies or other organizations successful.

Success in the case of private or public companies is measured in quality of products or services, growth, happy and satisfied customers, high employee satisfaction, and increase in sales and profits. We found 13 important attributes which ensure *success* in any *organization*.

Key Characteristics of Successful Companies and Organizations:

1. Effective Leadership: The Leaders can instill a sense of Common Purpose, usually by a Shared Vision Statement. Demonstrates High Integrity with strong Values and Beliefs. Ability to motivate people to work toward a common *goal* and ability to listen and see the *truth*.
2. Strong Values: Regarding what is Good or Bad, Right or Wrong. Integrity, Honesty, Consistency and Fairness among all Managers. These Values and Beliefs should be permeating to the lowest level.
3. Common Purpose: A unifying and Inspirational Shared Vision. Innovative and Creative Ideas free flowing on all Levels.

4. Commitment and Confidence: People Believe in and are Committed to the Objectives. They are Enthusiastic about completing their Assignments. They are confident about attaining their goals.
5. Well Qualified People: People are Good at what they Do. They are conscientious in finishing their Commitments. Quality is not compromised. Managers hire better people than themselves. Team members are dedicated to attaining excellence.
6. Open Communication: All layers of management are accessible. Communication is Open and Free flowing. Technical and Team communication are encouraged. Disagreements are accepted without loss of respect.
7. Superior Products and Services: Products and services are high quality, have exceptional utility, and meet real needs of the consumers.
8. Responsible Financial Practices: Regular Budget updates and at least yearly forecasting. Project and Cost accounting, Scheduling and Planning, Regular Financial reports and reviews. Careful attention to Cash Flow. Proper funding of all major functions.
9. Creativity and Innovation: Experiments and taking calculated risks are permitted. Positive attitude toward improvements. Accepting diversity and uniqueness in people. People are not afraid to make mistakes. People have freedom to act and have fun at work.
10. Decisive Organization: Minimum layers of management. People are challenged, decision making is pushed to the lowest level possible. Knowing that indecision is worse than wrong decision.
11. Customer Driven: Belief that all are working for the Customers, not Managers. Good understanding who the

customers are. Know what the Customer wants and why they buy the company's product.

12. Well managed Product and Market Strategy: Understanding of the overall aim, the strength, capabilities and weaknesses of the organization. Knowledge of Market, Customer, Industry, Technology and Economics. Clear concept on competitive positioning.

13. Long Term Orientation: Long-term thinking wins over expediency. Investment in training and education of people. Management seeks out the Truth in any situation. All relationships are managed for the long term. Customers, Employees, Contractors, and Business Partners are handled with genuine care.

I owe the courtesy to my highly respected Management Theorist, Dr. W. Edward Deming to at least paraphrase his 14 points every company and organization should follow:

1. Create constancy of purpose to improve products, and services in order to be competitive, provide jobs and stay in business.

2. Management must take on the worldwide challenge, responsibilities and take a leadership role for change.

3. Eliminate inspections and replace it with building quality into the products.

4. Move toward a single supplier for any one item on a long-term basis.

5. Constant improvements on all fronts; process, design, development, production and service, and thus decrease the costs of goods.

6. Institute on the job training and education.

7. Part of the leadership role should be to help people, machines, gadgets and do a better job.
8. Drive out fear, so everyone can work effectively.
9. Break down barriers so all departments can work as a team to solve any problems encountered in production or services.
10. Eliminate targets for perfection or unattainable production goals.
11. Eliminate work quotas, management by objectives, and substitute them with good Leadership.
12. Eliminate barriers that deprive hourly workers, managers and engineers of their rights to take pride of workmanship.
13. Support programs for education and self-improvement.
14. Transform the entire company and everybody's job to do better.

Meeting the above conditions ensures success in companies barring economic downturn that forces downsizing on all levels or in the worst case shutting down operations. This last resort usually applies only to small or start-up companies with limited financial resources or poor management.

- Systems designed, built or implemented by humans are inherently faulty and any imperfect system will be exploited sooner or later!

COMPANY OR ORGANIZATION FAILURES

Failures are the best teachers! My first company was very successful. We ended up selling it, later with many regrets, to a large corporation. The second start-up was a total failure but I learned more about running a business than anybody could teach me. Most entrepreneurs with at least one failure behind them would be more prepared and successful to run the next startup because of what they had learned from the past mistakes. Good examples are new restaurants where 90% fail in the first 5 years, those who try once more will succeed more than 50% of the time.

Most company failures can be attributed to leadership and management problems but there are failures totally outside the realm of the CEO's responsibility or any fault of management.

Here is my experience with a Start-Up entirely financed by a well established oriental company:

I had an excellent relationship with all the mother company's executives. Some of them already ran successful, productive, and profiting ventures or manufacturing facilities in the U.S. Our Business Plan was a joint effort and we would build a highly competitive high-tech organization to produce IBM PC-compatible computers and the required software: Operating System, with all important applications to be competitive and with some unique additions to have our own competitive edge.

The economic conditions were ideal, where most of the companies, including many Startups in Silicon Valley were well functioning or established, making profit and doing well. Therefore the business climate was close to optimum. This was the most difficult time to build new teams with the necessary expertise to achieve our business objectives. We needed the best and most experienced professional engineers which most other companies wanted to keep. I had to go outside of California's Silicon Valley and the USA, but worldwide to find these exceptionally well qualified people.

I had to hire about 75 professional engineers with the right experience to do the development process in earnest. It took me four months to find most of the staff but we had many delays and additional costs associated with getting the required legal papers and work permits for foreigners and moving these key individuals to the USA. I welcomed the mother company's help and their efforts when they found and hired a few managers for me: for the development of our peripheral drivers and manager of diagnostic program development, with my approvals.

I built up startups before, small companies and moved businesses from the East to the West Coast. I had hired at least 400 professional engineers and many hourly workers before but it had been easier than just hiring 45 under these circumstances.

Just as things began to fall into place I noticed some excessive dedication by two managers who were hired by the mother company's executives. They were very nice individuals and worked very hard handling a lot of contracts to acquire software, including proprietary drivers so we didn't have to take the time to develop them, rather just port the already well-tested software over to our new PC. They were the first in and the last out of the building and I was very impressed, until the first company picnic, where I met their wives. They were very attractive ladies, beautifully dressed, decorated with a lot of expensive jewelry, very sweet and very kind and each drove luxury sports cars priced about $100K or maybe more. I decided to check out the managers' references in case the mother company didn't do it. Where were they living, and the approximate salaries they were earning the past 10 years. To my surprise they lived in the richest section of town in over 5 thousand square-foot mansions which got my curiosity as their accumulated salaries would not be enough for even a down payment.

My suspicion grew to the point that I had to find out the story behind their financial success. When I asked them about their luck individually in casual settings, they appeared to be very defensive and each gave me a different story. One married a rich girl in Hong Kong, the other had rich parents, but when I asked them about their parents they would change the subject and never answer my questions.

I didn't want to talk to the executives at the mother company as they were the ones who hired them originally, so I expressed my concerns and suspicion to the company lawyers as we became close during the handling of all the legal papers about the foreign engineers and the many contracts we made with suppliers. When they asked what my suspicion was I told them; *industrial espionage*. They claimed I would have to prove it.

I decided to send one of the suspected managers on a business trip and asked one of my engineers to examine the files on his PC.

Not surprisingly, it was full of sensitive materials and proprietary software to which he was not allowed to have access, especially not to be stored on his personal PC.

Further examination and detective work showed that all the new information he gathered on his system was regularly transmitted to Chicago where the Hub was located for other industrial spies and there they gathered input from all over America and periodically the collected information was stored on magnetic tapes and these tapes were sent out of the country.

I contacted the US Customs and told them about the stealing of proprietary information but was informed that they can *not* check magnetic tapes and it is the best way to transfer any industrial or any other secrets out of the USA.

Without going into more details, my part of the company was shut down and I had to let all those knowledgeable and experienced people I just hired go. It was the saddest time in my professional career as many good people lost their jobs. Nobody went to prison, no-one was fined, only our facility was closed because the deal the mother company's lawyers were able to make with the government. I'm still disappointed on how this situation was handled on the political and judicial level. Unfortunately, this wasn't the last time the government and the legal department shortchanged the American people.

The Court handling of this situation reminded me of the Caltech incident in the late 1950s. One Chinese graduate foreign student sued the University for not letting him see certain Physics Notes and papers. The Judge took the student's side, but Caltech objected to the ruling and warned the judge that after making those documents available to the student, upon his return to China could build an Atomic Bomb in a few years. The judge ignored this warning and ordered the University to let the student have access to those papers. - A year later China detonated her first atomic bomb.

Ever since that incident, China more than doubled its efforts on industrial espionage and successfully copied ours and built its own Stealth Fighter before we fully tested ours. Even today, China seems to be the most successful country in acquiring American secrets on every level far exceeding the Russian efforts. They most likely have all the lost secret documents which disappeared, were deleted or were destroyed during past administrations and know more about government secrets than WIKILEAKS.

For Russia, the political influence is more important as in some cases their technology is ahead of ours and they can get most industrial secrets free from Americans who sympathize with socialism. The secret of "implosion" to start the nuclear chain reaction necessary for the atomic bomb was provided by a misguided American couple.

An example on USSR advantages on the technological side was not only in space, but was demonstrated to me by ex-KGB agents fixing a security related electro-mechanical part on my car for $50 that no American company could do without replacing most of the electromechanical components at exorbitant cost, well over $1700.

—∞—

I also want to mention another situation where a company regretfully failed. A new startup company hired me to bring a new project to fruition as they lacked experience in bringing system products, with three components (hardware, software and documentation) to market. We developed a communication control software package to transmit highly confidential encrypted information among banks on newly developed self-diagnosing modems. We would check the conditions of all components and lines within the network and set warning flags and notify the operators when it was time to swap out, diagnose or repair the unit or high-speed modems, including T1 carriers with any potential problems. All the hardware was designed and manufactured in a foreign country and we developed the software for them in America. This application package was very successful and our team was rewarded and treated very well by the top investors and the CEO.

The next project was faster (T2-T3 speed) and used newly developed hardware components with much more complex functions and additional product planning requirements. After writing the External Specifications based on customers, Product Planning and engineering input, I had to double my staff to have any chance of finishing the project on time. Unfortunately, we encountered many delays on all fronts where even tripling the staff could not provide all the functions marketing required for the promised date. After the heavy investments and the unforeseen delays I could not convince Marketing that we could not deliver the product unless we reduced the many features to the most important functions. Then update it with the frills product planning or the customers wanted at a later date.

This initial failure of mine eventually led to the closing of this company component and many good engineers also lost their jobs, including the stubborn heads of marketing and product planning. The Board removed the CEO and soon after they put in charge the VP who had never written a single line of code in his life to finish the application for the Network Control Project. However, I'm just as much to blame and I know I should have not given up on trying to persuade Marketing to cut back on the original set of requirements or delay the product release date by 6 months. My failure to save the project eventually resulted in losing the jobs of all those good people and the start-up company had to close its doors about a year later!

I made innumerable mistakes and had many failures in my life but I feel no regrets as I learned from each incident and never made the same blunder again. However, there was one failure that still hurts even after 60 years.

HIRING

My success I directly attributed to my teams, people I worked with and of course, including my secretaries. I was very lucky in hiring very good engineers, programmers, system administrators, and others. Our success I attributed to my previous experiences I had with employees given to me by my superiors or taking another manager's job with employees already in place.

In one particular situation I was exposed to a new, unwanted fix which resulted to be the most useful experience for me on how to build productive teams. This is what the Chinese call, "Setbacks just provide you new opportunities to excel."

At a company with over 300 thousand employees world-wide, my director gave me all the "troublesome" engineers (considered lazy, complainers, unhappy, dissatisfied, stubborn, argumentative) to get a new project started. I knew that my boss wasn't fond of me and this action proved it.

I was seriously considering changing jobs, but good fortune was on my side.

During my work at this company I volunteered and helped gifted students at the local high schools to find and develop their talents and improve their skills. One of my students I was mentoring insisted on me meeting his favorite teacher. The only time we could get together was after his lecture given after school hours to other teachers and parents, which very few attended. Luckily, I went, listened and learned a great deal about a new management tool to help improve productivity in students or employees that my earlier management training had not provided.

Using what I had learned during his presentation, I was able to make my raggedy team a top producer. I wish I knew who came up with the chart and methodology on how to make people more productive since that person(s) deserves a lot of credit. Below I summarize the process.

The entire process is based on the fact that one cannot change an individual's *personality* but one can change the person's *behavior*, especially with some authority or earned respect!

BEHAVIOR KEY TABLE

```
|     Constructive        | BEHAVIOR  |   DESTRUCTIVE                   |
|                         |   KEY     |                                 |
|_____|_____|_____|
| ACTIVE        | PASSIVE |           | ACTIVE      | PASSIVE           |
|_____|_____|_____|_____|_____|
|                                                                       |
|Ambitious      |    -    | Agressive |                                 |
|_____|
|High-Performer    |+Atitude | Confident |                              |
|_____|
^ |Good Performer    |+Conduct | Productive|                          ^
| |_____| |
| |Average Performer| Stable  | Secure    |                          | |
| | |_____|_____|_____|_____| |
| |                                                                   |
Encouragement                                        High expectation

Low expectation                                        Discouragement
| |_____| |
| | |                  |Attention | Pest   | Lazy       | |
| | |                  | getter   |        |            | |
| | |_____|_____|_____|_____| |
V | |                  |  Power   | Rebel  | Srubborn   | V
| |_____|_____|_____|_____|
|                    | Revenge  | Trouble| Negative   |
|                    | Maker    |        |            |
|_____|_____|_____|_____|
|                    | Disabled |   -    | Hopeless   |
|_____|_____|_____|_____|
```

The table above is centered on Behavior Keys in the middle, the left top block is relating to Constructive Behavior and the right side to Destructive Behavior. Both sides divide into two types: Active and Passive behaviors.

There also must be a good balance between Encouragement and Expectations for the Individual to be a Productive High Performer and the result of Low Expectations and Discouragement that typically put people on the Destructive side. A manager, teacher or parent can only change an individual's *behavior* while they are in *active* status. Therefore, managers, teachers, and people with authority, respect or rank must move the person from *passive* to *active* mode before their behavior can be changed for the better.

There are many important points for management to keep in mind while dealing with problem employees.

1. *Behavior cannot be equated to ability!* Example; unproductive and difficult employees may be very talented but unchallenging work assignments can make them feel belittled and they might become difficult to handle.
2. Expectation far exceeding *ability* is *discouragement.* If you assign jobs to do, for which person is unqualified, then this will make the person discouraged by showing some form of negative behavior.
3. Low expectations are destructive.
4. One can move a Constructive High Performer to a Destructive Troublemaker in one minute, but the reverse path takes much longer.
5. One must move the person from *passive* to *active* state before one can change the *behavior.*

Important steps for improving behavior and performance:

1. Identify and accept behavior.
2. Do active Listening.[11]
3. Look for potential (find good traits and capabilities).
4. Provide encouragement (based on good traits).

---

[11] It requires the listener to fully concentrate, understand, respond and remember what is being said.

43

5. Move the person from passive to active state via incentives (respect).
6. Balance expectations with abilities.

So I stopped looking for another job and instead I used the above management tool to make my team with all the ex-troublemakers high performers.

With Active Listening I built respect, using encouragement for positive attributes, I kept a good balance for each individual among expectations, encouragement and ability, only used constructive criticism; praise the good and just mention the fault. Incentives I tailored for individuals based on their need or motivation, such as: title, award, time off, power/promotion, authority, compassion, respect, attention, competition, challenge and recognitions.

—ᗯ—

New hires are a different game as one wants to pick the best for each job from the available pool provided by Personnel, Headhunters, Universities, Personal References, Advertisements, Internet or invited key people from other companies.

I paid particular attention to resumes since in addition to showing communication skills they should mirror personalities. Within minutes after the start of an interview one knows if the resume was written by the applicant or someone else. Granted, some new graduates needed help in writing a professional resume. Each resume should contain as a minimum the following: "What I want to do", "What are my qualifications for doing that job, Education, Experience, Extracurricular Activities, Awards or Recognitions and Additional Skills.

On a few occasions I was invited by universities to address the engineering classes just before graduation with BS and MS degrees.

Basically, I made up an overhead on different sizes of companies, their management style, what they look for in new hires, and the growth potential for the new hires. The chart below is self-explanatory but I will add a few comments for further clarifications:

COMPANIES

	LARGE	MEDIUM	SMALL	STARTUP
MANAGEMENT	Rigid	Some Flexib.	Dynamic	Volatile
Support	Yes	Mostly	Some	None
Tech Knowl.	Some	Some	Good	Little
Recognition	25%	50%	75%	99%
PREREQUISITE				
Experience	None	Some	Yes	Must
Comm. Skills	Written	Wr+Oral	Oral.+Wr.	Oral
Discipline	Must	Yes	Some	Should
Per. GROWTH				
Technical	Yes	Yes	Some	No
Professional	Yes	Maybe	No	No
Financial	10%	20%	30%	1%

The chart above will give freshly graduating engineers some understanding that without experience they should pursue large companies since they offer more opportunities for beginners to grow whereas smaller companies would be inappropriate for new graduates.

My original chart also included Consulting and Research companies where experience is also a big asset.

The financial growth is indicated as salary raises, but in the case of Startups the potential financial reward can be huge in the form of company shares when it goes public.

It is important to note that at Startup companies all employees must work extra hard and for long hours to ensure early product introduction, by being the first and using the shortest product development cycle as their financial backing is very limited.

- I never kept tabs on my work hours but my wife informed me that I spent in excess of 80 hours per week for 9 months straight at one of the Startups.

When interviewing people, professional, hourly or managers in any position I set the scene for free and fair exchange of information and ideas about each other. No desk or any object between us but open space where the entire body is seen. I paid special attention to keeping us on the same level without using any height advantage. Make every effort to put the person at ease in a comfortable setting to induce honesty and easy conversation. This way I didn't miss an important aspect of the interview; that was body language from eye contact to arm and leg positioning. I have only one important piece of advice for any candidate during an interview; *be yourself.*

Larger companies that can afford to take the time to train new employees are the best for new engineering graduates. For large companies I employed a different technique interviewing than hiring for small or startup companies. During the interviews I concentrate on personality and the required *abilities* along with the *right attitude.* Employees with good abilities and attitude could be trained to do great things for any company and themselves, and it is up to the managers to help make them productive. One wants people with positive attitudes, good abilities, innovative and with good problem solving skills in their respective professional fields.

With Small and Startup companies one must include the very important third attribute that is, the appropriate *experience*, as these companies do not have the financial means, or cannot afford the time to train individuals, therefore, it is essential that they have more than just the right experience for their assigned job. Often these individuals must fill in the missing parts of necessary work, which no-one is assigned or nobody is available to complete. Examples are many and here is one; if you're a hardware designer who needs help testing or a helping hand to use the test equipment - then regardless of your experience in design, the company cannot afford to hire people who need additional assistance, one must be totally self-sufficient.

Another requirement is the applicant's thinking style. In Startups a multidisciplinary type is preferred with a synthesist approach to problem solving. Unfortunately, most universities train their students to be only good analysts.

When hiring or promoting from within my organization managers, I preferred a mature and married individual with children. In my experience they were better in dealing with people's problems than singles or the ones who didn't have children. Bringing up your children provides added skills in dealing with problem employees, listening to complaints, noticing conflicts earlier among people, more patience, forgiving and understanding about unruly employees, and they are more likely to seek the truth. In short; they are more likely to recognize covered up abilities, as under everyone's hard shell there is someone who needs some understanding to be a productive team member.

Nowadays there are fewer and fewer married people with children because it is financially more advantageous to be a single parent because of the benefits they can receive by being unmarried or parents living separately. This new trend may destroy the family unit, which is the basic and necessary component for any healthy society. The other major disadvantage is for the children as the optimum environment for bringing them up is with mother and father raising them together.

- I heard during an indoctrination session by the communist party chief that the way to destroy the evil capitalist nations is by breaking up the families, changing the nation's history, ridicule religions, persecute or label the patriots, giving government run Healthcare for added control, provide free abortions and paint a beautiful picture of the future with promises for lots of free stuff. All this can be accomplished by recruiting socialist or communist sympathizers and Marxists in the education field, media, and entertainment industry to do the legwork for us.

Economically or financially it is no longer advantageous for young couples to get married.

—⚹—

On one occasion my company requested me to hire from their favorite universities and I was restricted to: Harvard, MIT, Celtech, Stanford, and Berkeley. Going outside those universities I had to have prior permission from the CEO. Fortunately, I was able to hire most of the engineers from those universities and only had to ask for permission to hire outside the preferred universities in a few cases.

Hiring fresh graduates, even with Masters or PhDs from the highest rated universities often ended in disappointment, as I found them unprepared or ill prepared for working in the industry. Many of them didn't know what a product was, what constitutes a necessary development cycle to guarantee user's satisfaction, or the importance of understanding what customers' needs are when designing products. They also failed to appreciate the necessity of high quality, the importance of specifications, documentation and design. Many of them lacked experience in testing, integration of components, planning, scheduling, cost considerations, timely decision making, teamwork, need for user documentation, etc. Basically, they all needed some training to get them started. In my experience, the University of Cal Poly prepared students for the industry; the real world in business planning, product development, and readiness to be productive right after company orientation. The runners-up were the MIT graduates since they adapted the fastest, in a few days after starting.

The following descriptions helped in understanding system product[12] development:

Building Blocks of System Product Development:

It is important to understand that each individual or company is a potential customer for products or services. Without Sales no profit can be made and without profit the company becomes unviable.

---

[12] System Products where three components are necessary for delivery to Customers: Hardware, Software, and User Documentation.

1. Company's View of a potential CUSTOMER:
   A) A potential BUYER   B) Have NEEDS and Desires
   C) Have some problems to be SOLVED

2. MARKETING Functions:
   A) SALES   B) Product PLANNING
   C) SUPPORT Customer base

3. ENGINEERING responsibilities:
   A) DESIGN and ARCHITECTURE to satisfy Customers' needs.
   B) SPECIFY the Design
   C) IMPLEMENT the Product
   D) TEST Internal and External Design
   E) Check Reliability and Effectiveness of the Product
   F) Make it AVAILABLE to the Customer

4. Main System PRODUCT Components:
   A) HARDWARE   B) SOFTWARE
   C) User Documentation

5. Customer's view of the Product:
   A) Availability   B) Effectiveness   C) Reliability

Good interviewing technique is the key to finding the best and filtering out the questionable characters. Usually, according to the applicants' resumes one doesn't find any unqualified professional engineers, so interviews and references are the only tools left to find the best fits. On a few occasions, I interviewed some very interesting people.

One Berkeley graduate with a MS degree in International Relations to whom I will refer as Mr. B. stands out and I remember well on how the interview went. Mr. B. was desperate to find a job since all his previous attempts for the past year had failed because he only wanted to work for non-profit organizations but at this point he was ready to make an exception.

In spite of his unique views on the real world he was very bright and spoke several languages. When I asked him why he didn't want to work for any business, his response was that they are immoral, take advantage of the employees and the customers, and their only interest is to maximize profit. I tried to explain that the reason we can hire and grow the business is because we make a profit. He admitted that the non-profit organizations where he applied for a job had no opening and don't expect to have one unless someone leaves, retires or dies.

When I suggested that he work for the government he thanked me for the suggestion, stood up and left. About a year later Mr. B. came back just to talk to me and told me that the government is also immoral as while businesses are out to make money the government is out to *waste* money.

He told me fascinating stories about the inefficiencies, duplications, political bias, mistreatment or lack of quality service to people who were supposed to be their customers. I was so impressed with his ability to recognize so many problems and even suggest possible solutions for each in a government run organization after being there only a year. I was ready to hire him in some capacity. He wasn't interested in changing jobs as he figured out that working for the government gives him the absolutely best salary and retirement package as long as the state keeps increasing taxes to cover the ever increasing retirement payments for the future. So he learned to live in the real world looking out for himself and accepted the fact that businesses must make profits in order to grow and prosper. Mr. B. came to see me one more time to tell about his new discoveries of corruption and potential solutions for eliminating foul politicians. I suggested that he run for office.

I had many interesting interviews like the above and when hiring at a VP or Director level, the CEO usually asked the same level management to also have at least an introductory meeting with the new potential hire as we must work together as a team to make the company successful. The new highly recommended VP of finance (CFO) made his rounds. After the CFO-to-be met with us individually we were called in by the CEO to voice our opinions. All six executives found the new person exceptionally qualified and approved his immediate hire with the only dissent from me.

My point was while he was technically qualified but I could not trust him in such an important position. My objection was ignored and the person was hired. Within six months he bled the company of at least $200 thousand by making unnecessary and unjustifiable contracts with his wife and family members.

My vote against hiring this VP cost me a lot of time and headache later as from that point on I had to interview everybody for any management position within the company that was interested in working with us.

I gave my managers the authority to hire on their own, but they always sent the likely candidates to be hired my way for my opinion before sending out the offer letter. I let my managers know what they should find out about the applicant during the interview and reference checks, but I didn't tell them how to

LEADERS! OR MANAGERS? AND DISCOVER YOUR TALENTS

conduct these sessions. My only request was that they also inform the potential hires of what their job entails and what they expect from them. I asked them to show the new potential hires the evaluation form out of courtesy, so they have a better idea on what measurements we use for each programmer or engineer. For example: Job Knowledge, Attitude, Quality of work, Planning and Organization, Scheduling, Communication, Teamwork, Design, Implementation, Testing, Components Integration, User documentation, and Support..

I also asked each of my managers before their yearly reviews to do a self evaluation and provided a form. The Self-Evaluation form was for all management personnel from supervisors to VPs, and of course for me as well.

Here are some of the Key questions on the form:

Do your direct reports know what is expected of them?
Do you authorize your teams to make their own decisions?
Do you give your reports the flexibility to learn from their mistakes?
Do you wrap the work assignment in a challenge?
Do you review people's performance more often than the yearly reviews?
Do you remind the people of the importance of their work?
Do you inform your people in time of the changes that affect them?
Do you know the progress made or delays in a timely fashion?
Do you really listen to all individuals in your group?
Do you solicit ideas or solutions to problems from your teams?
Do you give deserved credit and recognition for their accomplishments?
Do you encourage your people to grow technically or otherwise?
Do you provide training or guidance to individuals or teams?
Do you keep people accountable for what you expect of them?
Do you set a good example for your teams to follow?

53

Do you keep in touch with your direct reports on a daily basis?

Here I would like to add a few more cases of interesting interviews:

A young freshly graduated well qualified and bright engineer with a masters degree in computer science was escorted to my office by the hiring manager. Luckily he forewarned me that the only hesitation he had of hiring him was his name as he would have to interface with a lot of outside contractors and likely with customers, too. There is no way I would print his name as in English it was a vulgar and ugly expression with insulting meaning. So after the short introduction I popped the question, "Would you consider changing your name?" He immediately stood up and said, "No way, as I'm very proud of my name." To my surprise he knew the dirty meaning of his name in English but he didn't care. I still wonder if anybody else ever hired him with that name.

The only challenge I had during interviews were engineers who wanted positions which did not really suit them, or I had open positions where they would fit much better. I sometimes had to persuade them to change paths and try a different position in engineering.

One example stands out. A new graduate applied for an application programmer job. His attitude, outgoing personality, helpful well organized skills and talents, would much better fit the System Administration position. He gave in and accepted the new position providing he would be given the opportunity to transfer into the Development organization about a year later.

He is still in and enjoying his job as the Chief System Administrator and he will retire from that position. Surprisingly, he kept in touch with me after my retirement. Ten years ago he wrote me a thank you letter for putting him on a different path as he was very happy and found this type of job challenging. This type of work and responsibility used more of his talents and of course it was more satisfying and fulfilling.

Most of those I talked into a different path in engineering turned out to be happy and satisfied with the choice I helped them make.

Another interesting new candidate, a professor with a PhD teaching journalism who wanted a job in my company. He was bright, capable, and well versed in computer languages. I did end up hiring him and he performed very well. At the end of our interview I asked why he wanted to leave such a prestigious position in favor of a starting programmer job in the computer industry. His response still echoes in my ears every time I listen to the evening news or read a newspaper. He stated that he could no longer put up with the lax attitude in teaching journalism and training reporters. They no longer require a second source before reporting an event. The sign of a good news reporter is that the audience should not be able to tell which political side he/she is on. Nowadays one can easily tell the biased reporting on most of the news channels and I'm sure you can too.

Mark Twain words are still holding true for the media, "If you don't read the newspaper you're uninformed, if you do read the newspaper you're misinformed."

FIRING

In my line of work firing should be a last resort to remove a person from the team. There are other ways to encourage people to change jobs, assignments which would suit the person better within or outside of the company. Of course, there are exceptions.

On one occasion I inherited a large development group. In these cases I start by meeting every employee individually who would be reporting to me either directly or indirectly, as I like to find out the reasons for the failure of the previous director or VP. I was also seeking suggestions from each one for improvements. One programmer behaved very belligerently and only complained about the exempt employees not belonging to any unions. During further questioning I found out that he believed that his mission in life was to start a union for his fellow engineers. I simply told him that he must do that type of work after hours for now he must contribute and finish his assignments.

A few days later some engineers started to complain about him that instead of working with and contributing to the team, he constantly lectured them and so held up the team's progress. I invited him to lunch so I could find out what was really going on in a comfortable setting. He refused the invitation but was willing to talk to me in the conference room with his manager, supervisor and team leader present. I made it very clear that no more political talk is permitted during work hours and must carry his own weight in the development process. Unfortunately, he didn't listen and kept holding back the progress of the team. His contribution remained nil even after the third warning. With the help of Personnel we drafted and signed his separation papers and he was escorted out the door.

The next day the personnel manager came running into my office and pointed to the windows and asked me to look outside. I had three large windows facing the street. Right in front of my office marched about 50 people with red flags. The Personnel manager said they were demonstrating against me as they claimed I fired the guy because he was a communist. I told him that I never knew he was communist and I took the action because of his low performance and incompatibility with his teammates. His party affiliation would have been irrelevant.

The demonstrations lasted two more days with fewer and fewer people marching. To my surprise, my VP didn't believe me because of my background and he let me know it. I was shocked as he was already a millionaire making his money the capitalist way and he didn't seem to be the socialist type. When I came aboard he confided in me that he was divorcing his wife after a 25-year marriage for tax benefits. Before the divorce papers were filed he started to date one of my managers. Fortunately, about half of the 50 remaining employees reporting to me went to the VP office and told him they would all quit if he fired me. Of course, I felt my days were numbered in spite of my employees' support.

There were three more cases wherein I needed to fire employees I inherited but could not. I was told I cannot fire a black or a female person. However, one was caught by the night guard stealing PC's, so he got fired by the company, not me. The other, a lady, was found in the nude in the conference room after hours singing very loudly. After psychological evaluation the company was able to release her.

The third undesirable individual was the most troublesome as he was hired by the executive VP as a manager of OS (Operating System) development, reporting to me, just before I came on board. Because of his relationship with the higher echelons, my request to let him go fell on deaf ears. Even finding a much superior replacement from MIT didn't help convince the top. I often wonder if these high level executives ever realized the fact that the eventual company failure is partly attributable to their reluctance to let this manager, who they hired as a contractor go.

I wrote many recommendations for different reasons, but I could never write a letter like below where the manager obviously felt intimidated, enjoy:

Letter of Recommendation

1. Joe Smith, my assistant programmer, can always be found
2. hard at work in his cubicle. Joe works independently, without
3. wasting company time talking to colleagues. Joe never
4. thinks twice about assisting fellow employees, and he always
5. finishes the given assignment on time. Often he takes extended
6. measures to complete his work, sometimes skipping coffee
7. breaks. Joe is a dedicated individual who has absolutely no
8. vanity in spite of his accomplishments and profound

9. knowledge in his field. I firmly believe that Joe can be
10. classed as a high-caliber employee, the type that cannot be
11. dispensed with. Consequently, I recommend that Joe be
12. promoted to executive management, and a proposal will be
13. executed as soon as possible.

Addendum

This idiot was standing right behind my shoulder while I wrote this letter.

- Kindly re-read only the odd number lines.

TEAMWORK AND PERFORMANCE

What follows may be politically incorrect observations but I will tell the truth about my experiences even if it offends someone. It boils down to the fact that in many ways women engineers are better than men. For example, women tend to be better planners, schedulers, time managers, and are more likely to commit to and deliver projects on time than male teams. One can experiment on his own by assigning similar projects to women and man engineers and one could observe the differences in performance by using empirical data to measure progress and evaluate the end result.

Typically, women start on the project earlier while men tend to procrastinate. Women engineers tend to write better specifications. The women's teams communicate more often and discuss existing and potential problems among themselves while men tend to hold onto difficulties and problems until they are convinced that they cannot resolve them by themselves.

On occasions, in medium and large size companies, during a quiet time in the office, I assigned the development of programs to a man and a woman who had similar backgrounds, education and experiences. One experiment I like to mention because I got similar results to this type of assignment in most cases. I assigned the same program development to two freshly graduated students from CalTech. - By the way, at that time I was harshly criticized by upper management for hiring them with the same starting salary.

Both engineers estimated 4-5 weeks for completion. The lady finished the assignment on time, while the gentleman was 7 working days behind. This is what I found after comparing the two programs:

	Man	Woman
Documentation:		
External Specification	Specified all functions	Easier to read
Design Specification	Very Detailed	Bare Minimum
Operating Instruction	Bare Minimum	Very detailed
Lines of Coding:		
Assembly Language	None	None
Compiler language	Fewer lines	10% more
Performance:		
Time to execute	8.5 minutes	9 minutes
Number of Errors	2	1
User preference	NO	YES
Error messages	OK	Better

Because of the better operating guide and earlier availability the lady got the "YES" votes from the Users.

This example above is typical of what I found between male and female programmers/engineers but there were of course exceptions. Example: all women teams don't work as well as mixed teams.

TEAM BUILDING AND TEAMWORK

A major part of management responsibility is building productive *teams*. Once the Product Definitions are available and the associated projects with clear objectives, milestones, and goals are identified and established the team building begins in earnest with each team having their responsibilities to wit: schedule their own activities, complete their respective projects with checkpoints to measure progress. Of course, picking the right individuals with the right skillset, temperaments, mutual respects, and attitude likely ensure success.

The above items are easier said than done. They require you to know the individual contributors abilities and their relationship to one another. Finally, you must package the assignment or the design and implementation of all deliverables to both as a challenge to the members and also selling them on the importance of the entire project.

Usually, in my experience, the *plan* construction with the team leaders and the team members do the trick of properly wrapping the assignment, project or product in the most desirable light. This, I like to accomplish by using the Fishbone Diagram[13] wherein we define and answer the following questions: Who,

---

[13] Fishbone Diagram is a visualization tool categorizing potential problems and causes or used as a Planning tool.

What, Why, Where, When and the answer for How is left for the teams. I also found that it is imperative that the manager gets really involved in answering the Why? This is the opportunity to have the team understand the importance of their role, and the benefits of completing the high quality product or project on time for the customers' satisfaction. The answer to "why" must be inspirational, appealing and motivational.

Planning can also be done on a sheet of paper without using the fishbone diagram by answering the same set of five questions, and leaving the "How" definition to be written in the Specification after the design is done. Any completed *plan* exceeding a page without the answer for How, is a suspect for not being concise enough to be easily understood by the people involved.

What most of the Team Building presentations fail to tell us is the importance of team spirit, mutual respect and cooperation. They must work on every level in the company: Supervisors, Project managers, Managers, Directors, and VPs, and they *all* must work together as a *team* in order to ensure that system products meet the customer's needs and have an expeditious delivery with high quality.

The weekly status meetings are a good opportunity to keep everyone informed and keep open all communication lines on each level. However, these meetings tend to last longer than necessary, especially in larger companies and I'll cover meetings in general later.

Here are some experiences worthy of mention that I had as a team member, project manager, team leaders, manager, director or VP:

There are many variables in team members besides their capabilities and attitudes. The best working teams I found wherein the leadership role changes during the development process. For example; they chose one to lead the design phase, specifications, and documentation, then a different individual for setting the standards, the coding and testing, and another one for the integration phase of the project where all subroutines, error handling, programs and hardware had to interface harmoniously.

Thanks to large companies where one can observe and test many combinations of teamwork, I found that the most important aspect to a productive team is *mutual respect* among all members!

A surprising observation was that the most productive teams were one *man* and one *woman* with different ideas and approaches to getting things done but high respect for each other. They outperformed 3-5 members on all male or female teams! The only explanation I could come up with was: "viva la difference". It is not an accident that most successful children come from families with mother and father who despite their differences have high respect for each other and provide the optimum environment for their children.

Accordingly, the more differences there are between couples' abilities and talents the more they should be able to accomplish, providing they have a shared vision or purpose and genuine mutual respect. Therefore, if there is respect for each other, they can compensate for the other's weaknesses and combine each other's strengths effectively.

Please do not hire only women as that could present a bigger problem if you are not prepared for the possible complications and consequences. Instead, just make sure that all teams have some technically well qualified and respected female members.

Some of the complications I had seen and experienced are typically based on underestimating the power of women. Very ambitious and capable women have influence far beyond what most men can imagine and they will take advantage of any situation to gain control. They are especially successful if attractive. These women have more influence in family matters, morality, finance, religion, education and politics than just the number of votes they represent. This, I have experienced and seen. If fellow engineers, supervisors or managers don't recognize it and are unprepared, they might be used and sometimes in a sexual way.

For instance; the higher the position I attained, the smarter and more sophisticated young ladies tempted me whether they were married or not. In some situations their play acting seemed so sincere and polished that I failed to recognize the potential trap being set. On two occasions I almost succumbed to the temptations[14].

I had also seen many capable and ambitious women climb the ladder using their inherent talents to get close to the top at several companies. A few of these ambitious and successful women confided in me and explained how many more tools, advantages and power they have over men since the introduction of the birth control pills and the free abortion law was just an added protection in case they made a mistake. These tools helped them a great deal to get ahead if they liked their bosses. They have achieved more success now than ever before in human history. They also mentioned; if they

---

[14] See APPENDIX for some of my close encounters with the opposite sex at different companies.

didn't like their boss or he wouldn't cooperate, as a last resort, they could discredit or hurt him by claiming "sexual harassment" as you can always get a man to at least touch us, or if necessary we could just find another job at another company. - Obviously they lacked one of the very important attributes; *integrity* to be good leaders. One claimed that many women are attracted to men with good potential for advancements and not necessarily going after the big bosses. Not surprisingly, many of these ladies became very successful managers and caring bosses. So they did recognize their own talents and just wanted to get where they belonged fast and sometimes, with a certain amount of self-sacrifice.

My boss after his divorce married a coworker and she admitted to me that her original plan backfired after seducing him just to get herself a promotion. According to her, she taught my boss how to love, he was her best student and in turn she also fell in love with him. I hope she is still happy now and it wasn't only the money and the title she was after.

I should mention here that I had two lady bosses and one was a very good VP but the other one was very unhappy about her promotion and her management style proved it. She was promoted in the late 1970s when public companies had to show more women in management positions. A year later she left her job and soon after asked me to hire her as a contributor. She was a very smart and good engineer but not a manager type, and she knew it.

Besides the biological advantages women have over men like the complete pair of "X" chromosomes while man is missing half of his last chromosomes shown as "Y". This protects women from many health problems. For example: Color Blindness, Hemophilia, certain types of baldness, and there are other illnesses as well.

Women also tend to live longer, leaving men with the only advantage of physical strength and size. Women can also survive better under extreme pressure and difficult conditions. Good example is the Gulag where women survivors outnumbered the men every year in spite of having to perform similar duties, unless she was found to be very attractive by the prison officials, she would be used in a different way and provided with better food and accomodation.

I also found that men tend to exaggerate about their escapades, women tend to downplay their encounter with the opposite sex even if it was exquisite or completely satisfactory. Of course, she might share the truth with her closest girlfriends.

Please note, the great majority of women engineers were not as adventures like the few examples I mentioned above.

MEETINGS

Meetings are the most important tools for face-to-face communication among teams, or any other group of people. Many companies provide beautiful and comfortable rooms of different sizes to encourage and enhance face-to-face communications. However, this form of get together is often taken advantage of and overused especially if it is not planned or conducted the proper way.

There are many types of meetings but I'll combine two: *status* and *decision* making.

Here are some suggestions to improve the effectiveness of your meetings:

The secret of effective communication is not how much, but how little time it took to convey or understand the message!

Status meetings should be scheduled at regular intervals, like weekly or more often when necessary.

Prepare an agenda and indicate starting and ending time.
Identify the people who need to attend and invite only those.
Invited people must send a representative if they cannot attend.
Have someone take notes to be published after the meeting.

Have a set time for each subject and topics discussed.

Table all discussions that are not related to the meeting's objectives.

Prepare the meeting room and start on time.

Seating arrangements are helpful when opposing views are likely.

Solicit everyone's input in decision making meetings. (I usually get the best input from those who are quiet and afraid to speak!)

At the end of the meeting summarize the conclusions reached.

After the meeting, publish a summary report.

When taking over responsibilities for other executives or directors I often had problems associated with meetings. Here are some of the problems and potential solutions.

1. Starting on time - Put a sign up, "Do not disturb" and lock the doors on the inside within 1 minutes after the starting time.
2. Lasting too long - I had the chairs removed.
3. No show and no designee - Invited his secretary or one of his reports, usually the most junior contributor.
4. Latecomers - Had to publish the Summary Report.
5. Uninvited Guest - I asked them to return to their offices.

Usually after a few weeks my meetings started and ended on time and people adjusted very well. People do what is expected of them, so be clear and communicate your expectations of them.

For my decision making meetings I always invited Larry, who was a devil's advocate. One of my new managers came to me after a few meetings and asked me to stop inviting Larry because he disagrees with every decision we want to make. I told him that when we disagree and he offers alternatives we will always look at the other side or another solution, therefore, I see him as an asset to help us make better decisions.

MANAGING PEOPLE

*M*anagement is necessary and everyone must do it whether one has that title or not! The workers or contributors must manage themselves, their assignments, schedules, commitments, behaviors and their relationships to each other and the team. Therefore, *to succeed in life one has to be a manager, regardless of where the person stands on the totem pole.*

Supervisors and team leaders must also guide and sometimes manage the individuals reporting to them. Managers and directors are usually sandwiched in between the lower and upper echelons. For some reason, I never had any serious problems below or parallel with my title which I attribute to the fact that I treated everyone as a professional regardless of their place in the hierarchy from the cleaning people to the top. For many reasons the upper management was the more difficult to deal with. I often reported to people who had no idea what we were doing but only cared about the timely delivery of the product and on occasions not valuing the importance of the product quality aspects enough.

There were only two groups of people who really challenged my management skills; the Research Department and the Publication Group.

Firstly, in the Research group everybody had a PhD and their individual mannerisms and attitudes toward each other were unusual. Many of them wanted to be the smartest in the group or wanted to get special credit and recognition for their work, contributions or ideas. Others were introverts, making communication and teamwork difficult, even discussing esoteric or out of world ideas were troublesome. In spite of their uniqueness and unusual mannerisms, they were excellent problem solvers and contributed a great deal of ideas for new and advanced products.

Secondly, in the Publication department - I had many problems unique to this group, unlike other departments I had encountered. I guess they were artistic people without much discipline and had the hardest time to keep to schedules, including coming to status meetings prepared and on time. However, they proved to be the best actors, organizers and entertainers during company picnics.

INDUSTRY VS. STATE GOVERNMENT OPERATION

We, as experienced managers and directors in the industry, were invited by a State Government to review and improve the effectiveness of the State Capitol operations. I was assigned to work with the Director level and up to provide guidance, help, and assistance and introduce new management tools.

We were restricted to one 2 hour session per week for 12 weeks. I also had to learn their methods of operation first before I felt qualified to recommend any improvements. To be accepted by and have real cooperation from the other directors or VPs was essential, so I prepared as much as I could before my first meeting.

In a company setting I would sit down with each of my employees or direct reports individually but in this case I had to change to a questionnaire to learn from them because of the shortness of time.

My questions all fitted on a single sheet of paper leaving room for answers and contained the following:

First name
Title

Responsibilities and Function

To whom do you report to, title and responsibilities?

Who pays your salary?

How long have you served in the current position?

How many direct reports do you have or attach your organization chart?

What are your difficulties?

What suggestions do you have for improvements?

If you had a choice of what position would you like to have?

Who are your customers?

What is your required input?

What is the process and the output of your department?

At the initial meeting to get acquainted, we agreed to convene every Tuesday from 4 to 6 PM. After the self-introductions I handed out my questionnaire to be completed for our first officially scheduled meeting the following week. This first official meeting was very cordial, and went very smoothly as we talked about many things including their concerns. I was impressed by everyone, their communication skills, demeanor and professional comportment. They all seemed to be eager to know about my background and whether I could be of some service to them. After answering all their questions they all seemed to be satisfied and they recommended not to spend too much time on my learning their operations, instead to describe experiences relevant to their operation, provide management tools, make suggestions to improve their quality and productivity. However, of the original 17 people attending about half of them left at 5 PM with seemingly valid reasons, among them: carpooling and picking up kids. Fortunately, they were all bright and capable people so we could reduce the meeting's duration to 70 minutes instead of 2 hours.

My first shock came while reviewing the returned questionnaires. For example: no-one knew who *paid* for their services, no-one really knew who their *customers* were, no-one knew who paid their *salary*. Basically, everyone believed they worked for their bosses and were paid by the State!

It took considerable effort to convince them otherwise or have them realize that they were supposed to work for their real customers, the *public* and their paycheck was covered by the *taxpayers* as governments have no money until they take it from the wage earners or from company profits. Once it became obvious to all that they should be working for their customers, not their bosses, things started to work out fine and I was able to extend the lecture time up to 90 minutes. From this point on their cooperation and wanting to learn new tools, methodology to deliver high quality service for the public was amazing. A few of the directors seemed to be feeling guilty about not knowing for whom they were really working and who were their real customers. After our meeting some of those individuals approached me and pointed out a lot of red tape, duplication, bureaucracies, and decisions made based on getting political benefits. I was amazed by their honesty and things turned out to be even more inefficient than what I had imagined.

By the 10th meetings they were all sold on wanting to streamline, improve their services with smaller staff and much smaller budget. They were ready to incorporate all that they learned and as a matter of fact cooperated with lowering their budget requirements and making the State Government a more efficient organization. They set the plan, methodology and strategy in motion for applying them to all the staff in all departments.

The next meeting was combined with the entire staff, filling up the largest room in the Capitol with several hundred workers attending. Their plan for the transformation was presented and well received by all, only the starting date had to be established by the superiors. I should also mention at this point that during my meetings with the department heads other experienced managers gave parallel lectures, so this education was done on all levels for all employees at about the same time frame.

After the general meetings we were asked to consult with the Legal Department and the employee Union chief. They both objected to the immediate start of the transformation process, the Union guy estimated that up to 30% of employees may have to be let go eventually and the entire capital budget reduced to half if the plan is fully implemented. We of course set him at ease that instead of letting employees go we just stop hiring and let the natural attrition rate bring us down to the needed levels. The Legal Department, however, did not permit and would not approve a starting date for the transformation to begin.

Since the Legal Department refused to give us the reason for the objection we went to the State Attorney General whose secretary explained that this is the wrong time to start such a project with such great potential and expected highly beneficial results as the success will be credited to the currently elected Governor, who wasn't representing their party. - That time the thought occurred to me that all outside contracts must be approved by this Legal department so one can guess who might be the most likely recipients of these lucrative contracts.

Not all was lost as Personnel would change the new employee orientation to include their responsibilities and quality service they should provide for the true customers, the people of the state.

This incident taught me an important lesson and the memory remained with me for the rest of my life. From that point on before voting for any candidate of this party that stops progress and cheats the American people I double check the qualifications of the candidates. This was another example of the corrupt justice that does not work for the people of the State, but the party they represent!

There is no way I want to specify which State Government we tried to improve but you're welcome to guess from the following list of states where I have worked: Alabama, Arizona, California, Connecticut, Florida, Louisiana, Nevada, New Jersey, New York, Oregon, Texas, and Utah.

My conclusion was and is that anything the government does for us costs at least twice as much as it should and also takes longer than necessary. Also, there is no way any private or public company could survive with the same inefficiencies found in most government organizations! Government has no ideas about downsizing or having a lean organization while companies must adjust to the economic conditions and to the marketplace, the government keeps growing and spending more in any conditions. - There should be a legal or other mechanism for limiting the size and power of governments.

I experienced as a young man what Thomas Jefferson said with some variation in parentheses, "A government big enough to give you everything (they promised) you want, is strong enough to take everything you have."

—m—

I recalled some of our discussions about government jobs I had with Mr. B. whom I met the third time for lunch. According to him, the most lucrative positions to have are in the government and especially to be elected representatives all the way upto and including senators. After they take their oath to uphold the constitution and serve its citizens, many of them take another oath, right after the first one, to start serving themselves and the party they represent. The many advantages, special treats and benefits they receive not only from the State but also from lobbyists that can make them rich. The best features are the retirement benefits and the low-cost healthcare lasting for a lifetime. Mr. B. also pointed out that government employees are paid considerably more, sometimes twice as much as equivalent jobs in private industry. - It is true.

Mr. B. has changed his perspective on the real world just about 180 degrees and became a fan of Ronald Reagan and recited his words, "The government is like a baby's alimentary canal, with a happy appetite at one end and no responsibility on the other."

Mr. B. also assured me that there are good people in the government who are honest, hard-working and doing a good job for the benefit of the people of the state and the country. - I consider them the leader types and hopefully they will be often promoted to higher positions regardless of their party affiliation.

MANAGERS OR LEADERS

My experience and observation show that individuals with natural leadership talents deserve a different type of training than people with just aspiration to be managers. While many managers have leadership skills few of them could qualify as a good natural leader.

The selection process to distinguish between manager and leader types is a challenge but here I'll offer some suggestions. In my management training classes I tried different questions to be answered by the participants at the beginning of the lecture series in order to find ways to distinguish between the naturally talented leaders and just ambitious bright manager types. Of course, I told them that this is not homework but it will help me to understand the individuals in my class to tailor my presentations. Thanks to the participants, a great majority of them obliged and answered my questions.

I found the answers to the following questions to be the most revealing about a person's thinking style, leadership qualities and problem solving skills.

Based on the answers I received on my questionnaire I could determine the individual's talents and I came up with a potential entrance examination to qualify people to the more advanced Leadership training.

1. First assignment was to write a recommended solution to a problem the attendee feels very strongly about, but not to exceed half of a page. Next time I returned the page and asked them to write a well prepared valid opposite view or contradicting argument on the other side of the page. - After reading both sides of the paper one can easily discern whether the individual is willing to deal with and accept opposite views in real life.

2. Second assignment was to present a written scenario for solving a current complex problem such as water shortage, pollution, illegal immigration, global warming, overpopulation, hunger, homelessness, drug addiction, if the attendee was a dictator with unlimited authority and power.
    - By reading the methodology and proposed solutions one can easily tell whether there was a good grasp on the complexity of the problem requiring additional experts or a team to solve it, the problem solving skills and ability to think broadly, wisely. One can also see whether the individual is considering the effect and timing of the proposed solution on the people and nature, and how progress is measured.

3. The third is another hypothetical question, "What would you do if you inherited a billion dollars?" - From the answer one can determine the responder's understanding of the real world and whether it is interested in the way to help self and family only or many others as well.

4. Fourth assignment; if you could improve anything in this world what would be the first 3 things you would do? - From the answers one can conclude what the individual thinks are the most important problems to be solved and their priorities, and the breadth of understanding of the world we live in.

I had tried giving other assignments to people attending my classes and lectures but with limited success. However, the most varied and interesting answers I received were for the following question, " What would our world be like without religion (organized or individual beliefs)?" To my surprise, very few people provided a written response, but everyone else wanted to participate and explore the possibilities in a group discussion during or after the class. The after class discussion was so interesting that I recommend this question to be used in group settings at schools and universities - we can all learn from the views of others.

Of course, leadership talents should be identified in any individual as early as possible in order to save them from being reprogrammed. An example is the many bright people who choose to become lawyers. The training they receive is contrary to good Leadership as they become Followers of Law. Timely decision making is replaced by arguments, questioning everything, whether they end up on the defense or offense (persecutor) side of the fence. For them, integrity might be more of a handicap than a desirable trait. As a result, the more lawyers in the government the slower the government works.

During some of my management training sessions I also asked a 5th question, "What is the purpose of the organization chart?"

Out of many good answers I received I never encountered the most important use of organization charts for management. For me, and I let them know, its primary function is to show the path on how far down one can delegate the decision making process.

Based on my experience the people I found with leadership talents tended to be pragmatists, forging ahead without or minimal party affiliation, value time, not afraid of making timely decisions, with a certain amount of entrepreneurial drive, motivator, a people person, challenger, good understanding of dependency on teamwork to accomplish things of value for others, and knowing their own *strengths* and *weaknesses*. - Definitely not the lawyer types.

Personally, I could not vote for any representative running for Congress who has a Law degree and practices law! I agree with Thomas Jefferson, *"Congress errs in too much talking, how can it be otherwise in a body to which the people send one hundred and fifty lawyers, whose trade is to question everything, yield nothing, and talk by the hour?"*

Talk is cheap … except when Congress does it.

The more lawyers elected in the government the slower and more inefficiently it works.

Interestingly, based on the answers I received on my questions I encountered a few candidates with real leadership talents and potentials but lacked ethics, fairness and moral training. An example was solving the homeless problem, one of the participant solutions required either seizing all second homes or extra taxing of the rich to provide housing for the poor. He obviously lacked home or school training about robbing Peter to pay Paul which is never a good solution. Therefore, Ethics training should be required in schools. Just imagine, these types of people with leadership talents but no integrity or good moral values, could become bank robbers, pirates or outlaws who distribute the stolen goods to the poor and become popular heroes.

If one is considering a career in organized crime, forget about the private sector, join the government, they almost never go to jail.

TECHNICAL BACKGROUND

G etting promotions often satisfies the need for feeling important, but for me it was quite different, instead, I felt more complete in the sense that I used more of my talents for the benefit of others as I always was a people person and team player.

As an engineer or contributor I enjoyed a challenging career. My first programming experience was writing business applications on Univec II using assembly language, followed by diagnostic programming, peripheral and system interaction testing for banking systems using both machine code and assembly languages.

In those days programming was considered more of an art than a science and some companies hired linguists instead of engineers. In the diagnostic programming field we had to understand the nitty-gritty parts of the logic, small components of the computers, "and" and "or" gates, switches, diodes, transistors, the hardware and use machine language, and sometimes entering commands bit-by-bit in the processor. We only had core memory, drums, tapes, paper tapes and a little later fixed head disc for storage. The discs with fixed heads were faster in recovering or storing data than processors could handle, so we had to store and read data in an interlaced fashion.

The many electromechanical peripherals were difficult to test, like check sorters for banking and later post office applications as it was hard to tell what failed, the program or the mechanical parts.

Here I was introduced to the first multiprocessor system using Algol language doing Matrix calculations. (Note : Algol was the predecessor of all advanced compiler languages. After Algol came language B followed by C and then even the currently used C+ and C++.)

Possibly the most satisfying programming assignments were writing Process Control applications as I could use most of my technical background like Chemistry, Nuclear Engineering, Physics, Thermo Dynamics, Transformation, Algebra, Logic and Mathematics. However, no Software Engineering methodology was used in program development. The result was that slowly and surely errors in software, known as "bugs" became more prevalent and were considered a necessary evil by some. I remember when two hardware engineers were asked in a programming class what methodology they used to write a perfect driver without "bugs". They looked at each other and proclaimed, "We didn't know errors were allowed." I had to use their philosophy on the most challenging programming assignment as people's lives depended on it. We had to write an auto-pilot program so it would be possible to land an aircraft in case the pilot gets disabled saving his/her life and the expensive plane. There it occurred to me that more discipline must be used in designing, writing and testing programs. Later, as manager of program development, I started classes for error-free coding methods before the formal Software Engineering methodology was introduced. I also introduced guidelines and standards for the set of documentation required to produce high quality system products and to ensure customer satisfaction, such as: Product Requirements, Functional or External specifications, Internal Design, Coding standards, Error handling, Product component Integration Plan, Testing both Design and Functions, Stress and Negative testing.

Next I enjoyed using the BASIC compiler language for small applications, but FORTRAN was a disappointment after using the more advanced ALGOL before. I had to write many Fortran programs like processing microfiche and testing plotters. The least enjoyable was doing Operating System maintenance on large mainframes where one had to figure out how the original creator of the program was thinking when it was written in assembly language code after using more advanced compiler languages. But here, I was introduced to e-mailing, measuring large system performance, communication networks, the MULTIX operating systems developed at MIT, which and in parts ended up as UNIX operating system at Princeton University. Of course, it was disappointing to me that MSDOS won out as an Operating System on Personal Computers instead of UNIX.

Outside the office activities were mainly sports, coaching teams, tutoring mentally gifted students and teaching foreign languages.

I also enjoyed many interesting and challenging assignments in the military, such as language translations, encryption, decryption, problem solving, tactical exercises, training, strategic moves on battlefields, handling POWs, briefing, debriefing, interrogation methods, survival training, and developing computer system security programs and procedures.

Designed, developed and presented both technical and management training subjects. Also, worked with and helped different organizations in the transformation process to Total

Quality Management. Some of my lecture topics in order of popularity based on grading on the returned evaluation forms from the audience:

Software Estimation
Project Management
Software Development Management
Nuts-and-Bolts of Software Management
Software Quality
Software Project Sizing
Measuring and Improving Software Quality
Improved Management Techniques
Successful Organizations
Nuclear Reactor Cooling Systems and Safety
Function Points
Product Development Cycle
Documentation Flow
Software Product Specifications
Product Testing Methodologies .

CONCLUSIONS

My theory on *leadership*, based on my experiences, is that it requires special talents and those abilities are often inherited and may show up early, even in childhood in some form.

Top notch leaders do things to *benefit others* and they *plan actions* to improve people's lives and welfare with a positive and inspiring *vision* for the future.

I also believe that the Franklin Reality Model is an important tool for understanding self and others, and also helps identify good Leaders.

People with inherent talents for leadership deserve special training to become more effective and better leaders.

People with genuine leadership talents should be identified as early as possible and provided with special training because we need more of them in today's world with many complex problems to be solved.

Some of the training subjects should include training in Business Ethics, Morality, Fairness and Integrity. Provide them with other management tools as well so they can make a positive difference in the world we live in.

In nature, leaders can learn from a marching wolfpack. The front of the pack are the old ones who know the way and set the pace, followed by a few strong ones to protect the front. In the middle are the young and the weak, protected in the rear by a few strong ones. The last one is the *leader*, the Alpha male to make sure no-one is left behind. Good *leadership* is not necessarily being in the front, but more importantly, taking care of your team!

—⁓—

Problem definition and problem solving skills are other weak points for mostly everybody as profound knowledge is not developed in schools. Profound knowledge is the skill of knowing or predicting the outcome or potential results of events or actions. In our world most knowledge exercises, games, training or TV shows are based on developing the ability for fast recall. It is not enough to have a photographic memory if some else can recall it faster. Possibly the most popular show along this line is Jeopardy but it has no relationship to *knowledge* but only ability to recall. I wish there would be knowledge based game shows where the contestants are asked such as, "What would happen in case of mixing Hydrogen and Oxygen?", or "If we convert our monetary system to be gold based", "Allow Charter and Trade Schools to compete with public schools", "Stop Illegal Migration", "Dam up every river", "Do away with Political Correctness", "All laws passed by the Congress would equally apply to them as well", or "Provide more opportunities to American Indians stuck on Reservations".

- Some of us are blessed with a photographic memory, which is useful, but in my case I'm always out of film.

Another important need for solving problems is understanding the *system* as many of the problems we deal with on a daily basis can be so complex that no single individual could have a complete grasp of it. Therefore, most complex problems would need a team approach to properly define, understand the system where it can be applied and should work and have a good chance that the proposed solution will truly solve the real problem.

Understanding the *limitation* is another key component for solving problems as all improvements have dependencies and limitations. One must also have a good method to *measure* and evaluate *progress* so the proposed *solution* can constantly be improved and monitored.

There is even a psychological aspect to Problem Solving as the proposed Improvement must be sold to the people who are affected both on the implementation and recipient sides. Also, the team or individual often needs *authority* to execute the proposed solution.

In problem solving the last thing to consider is the money as most good solutions typically save money and time.

Can you imagine asking for problem resolution in the government without politicians asking for more money or higher taxes to solve it? Any politician asking to increase your taxes without defining the real problem, the proposed solution, the expected outcome, the affected areas and people, how to measure progress and results, and justification for the added money should be impeached.

As P. J. O'Rourke said, "Giving money and power to the government is like giving whiskey and car keys to teenage boys."

Problem definitions often require investigation for tracking down the true origin of the problem. The often used example is the "oil-leak" in a car. After asking "why" several times might lead you to find that the real cause was the use of an inferior quality seal which was introduced as a cost-saving measure by a company employee. So it was not sloppy workmanship in placing the seal or bad oil changing practices.

Another example is the humanitarian crisis at the Mexican border. If you ask "WHY" just a few times it becomes obvious and evident that the *real source of the problem* is the unsecured border. If we had a secure border, we would not have to deal with hundreds of thousands of illegal immigrants and their families.

I have lived and worked in at least four countries and visited at least ten others, but I found the United States of America to be the best place by far. The freedom, opportunities, the people, the beauty of the land and the great Constitution of this country are beyond valuation. However, in the spirit of "there is always room for improvement" I offer some suggestions.

Areas which need expeditious improvement are: Public Education (at least it should have some competition from Charter and Trade Schools), illegal Immigration is destroying legal immigration (there is no safe Country without Secure borders), Legal System - prisoners should be able to work and pay at least their own keeps and expenses (don't put this additional burden on taxpayers).

All able bodied men and women should serve at least six months in uniform and have the basic military training as in Switzerland, as it would help our young people more than any other social program devised by politicians.

Instead of debate classes, teaching teamwork, debate requires adversary positions and is not conducive to problem solving, productive work or learning.

My brother traveled all over the world and visited 91 countries mainly for business. After his retirement he was surprised to see so much discord, dissatisfaction, riots, demonstrations, and complaints by women, and young people in the USA. His conclusion was, "Our schools must be teaching the wrong history and another country's Constitution as everyone else in the world would like to come here." He explained that every country he visited many individuals approached him for help in getting them into the USA. In Muslim countries, mostly young women, in poor countries young men, in developed countries both men and women. He added, " The poor in America are envied by most people around the globe, as they often have more than the rich people in many other countries."

Those who criticize this great Representative Republic without offering improvements, solutions or recognizing its good qualities should be sent to any other country to live there for a year. I bet over 95% would want to return here and would become a better American.

EPILOGUE

Continued from Prologue, for the retirees:

My mother used to say, " It is not the honey that makes your tea or milk sweet but the stirring!" So start stirring up a storm, be proactive in stimulating minds and prompt people to act on and solve problems in our technical, social, physical, and spiritual world.

Children are the seeds of the future. Plant love in their hearts and sprinkle them with wisdom and life's lessons so they can grow up in harmony with their spiritual, physical, mental and emotional selves - all have to be balanced to be pure and healthy.

I heard from some of you old folks that the American education system failed our youth because they don't know our history, Constitution, and have little understanding of the real world. Some of you blame the schools, teachers, unions, parents, universities (where the liberals professors outnumber conservatives 12 to 1), the news, media and the entertainers. However, maybe we, the old folks, failed to tell our children and grandchildren or share our experiences; good or bad. Perhaps, we should have stepped in and helped them to reach maturity with higher moral standards, critical thinking, being responsible, integrity, better problem solving skills and wisdom to counteract the bad influences.

My question to you, "What did you do to augment or correct our weak but one of the most expensive public education systems in the world?"

I strongly believe that Civilizations should be graded and measured based on how we treat Nature, each other and how we prepare the future generation to lead and love the world.

It is *not* too late! Get involved at least with your grandchildren so they can learn and know the truth about real life, economics, finance, religion to give them a moral compass, politics, history, ethics, geography, being responsible for their own actions, and other important things such as *integrity*.

There are too many young people who believe in or want socialism as they don't know any better. Socialism is the curse of humanity and cancer of society. I know I was lucky to have survived several variations of "socialism" from Hitler to Stalin.

Save the nation from plunging into a disaster despite the pervasive liberal and Marxist propaganda which always failed its people as history proves.

Also teach them the only *three main responsibilities* for any government:

1. Protect the country and its people (Military, Secure borders, CIA)
2. Provide internal security (Police, Justice system, FBI.)
3. Provide the environment for all its citizens to be able to prosper and grow (Infrastructure, Transportation, Banking, Schools and Education opportunity, Freedom of religion, Safe Monetary practices.)

The rest of the niceties are secondary and not to be given until the three top priorities are satisfied!

Who wants to live in a weak state, insecure and poor country?

Some of you blame the politicians, the Congress, the President, but we elected them as the majority of the people don't know any better. We should have a program to discourage voting by irresponsible people. Our education system will not teach critical thinking, conflict resolution, integrity, ethics, special problem solving skills, profound knowledge, or respect for the elders. etc.

If we're ever going to change the down spiral of our nation, we must come to grips with just how far we have fallen.

A few examples:

- When LBJ's "War on Poverty" began, less than 10% of children were growing up in a single parent household. Today, that number is over 35%.
- In 1950, less than 5% of all babies in America were born to unmarried parents. Today, that number is over 40%.
- The poverty rate for households of married couples is less than 7%. For households which are led by a female single parent, the poverty rate is now close to 38%.
- The American students are rated 75th in the world out of 110 countries, yet we have the most expensive public education systems in the world, over $8000 per child.
- Students in schools cannot read the Bible but can in prison.
- I also saw Hitler's socialist party's "Brown-shirts" behaved in a much better way than the American ANTIFA organization!

A challenge for you; we tend to measure most everything; loss, hurt, pain, accidents, damages, divorce, sports, disasters, happiness, etc. with a $ sign attached. There must be a better way and what is it?

Most scholarships should go to support students in the field of science as sports and arts combined provide less benefit for the future of our nation.

It is never too late to get involved, to improve education and share your experiences and teach your grandkids about real life. The now-generation cannot fathom the hardships the parents had to go through to survive.

After sharing some of my experiences, I sincerely hope you will share yours too, especially if you're already retired.

—m—

Just for fun:

I have always been interested in human behavior and human nature, therefore, with my friend we developed games to trick people and observe their behaviors. For example:

My friend and I went to the secretarial pool where at least a dozen ladies worked serving the entire company of hundreds of engineers and programmers with typing mostly specifications, and we asked for all the nickels they could muster. They of course were curious as to why and we obliged by fibbing that the cigarette machine failed and instead of a quarter it gives you a pack for a nickel. - Within an hour, downstairs where the cigarette machine was, most of the secretaries with their bosses or boyfriends were in line trying to get a pack for a nickel, even those who didn't smoke. We had a good excuse as we timed our trick right after the cigarette machine was restocked and we claimed they must have fixed it. We repeated this trick with the coke machine at another company and it worked the same way. People who didn't drink coke still went to try to get one.

What are *your* conclusions about these experiments?

On one occasion our trick backfired when in front of one of our gullible colleagues we made up a scheme around making $50 thousand dollars by importing a special medication from China which could be brought in by a diplomat without paying duty and it was very expensive and in high demand in the US. The following week, again in front of the same college, we congratulated each other and split the $50 thousand dollars between us using fake money we received from the bank for testing money counting machines. - That year both of our tax returns were audited and we had a hard time explaining that we just played a trick on our colleague and had to show some money samples to prove that our excuses were true.

- So what conclusions did you draw from the experiments above?

APPENDIX

MY FAMILY EXPERIENCES ON ELIMINATING LEADERS

Since 1943 March 19 the Nazi Socialist party (Arrow-Cross) gained supporters mainly from the German sympathizers in my country. Many were from the German-speaking minorities who settled in Hungary after the Muslims were pushed out as they left a huge amount of land totally depopulated thereby opening up fertile lands for newcomers. The indigenous Hungarian population was killed or taken slaves by the Turks.

My father had a high position, Chief Financial Advisor for the government. He was deeply troubled by the ever-increasing Nazi influence in our country. Initially, only the political influence seemed to gain some momentum, but the situation became desperate when the German Army invaded Hungary. The Nazis arrested and took our Regent Horthy to Germany and they gained complete control of our land and government. We knew that the reason for the invasion by the German Army, the arrest of our Regent, and replacing the government leadership with Nazi sympathizers happened because of the Gestapo found out about Hungary's highly secret attempts to get out of the war and side with the Allies. Regent Horthy did everything possible to get Hungary out of the war and join the Allies. Unfortunately, the allies were reluctant to accept our appeal as they were afraid it would trigger an immediate invasion of our country by the German Army. This turned out to be a poor decision by the Allies as the German Army invaded us anyway. From the Allied side, there were not enough considerations given to the 15 million Hungarians and the 850 000 Jews who were safe until the puppet pro-Nazi government took control.

The Nazis immediately started to ship the undesirables to concentration camps. Before the war was over, they were able to transport about 430,000 Jews and dissidents to Germany, and out of those 92,000 never returned to Hungary. Many of them perished or they didn't want to return to their home and settled in some other Western countries.

To our surprise, the socialist Arrow-Cross party leaders ignored us at the beginning, in fact when the Romanians changed sides and made a pact with Stalin to receive the eastern part of Hungary for fighting on the side of the Red Army, a high-ranking German officer gave my father ample warning, so we could escape in time and move West, away from the invading Romanian and Russian forces.

My mother and father had already experienced the Romanian invasion of Hungary after WWI. The Romanians imprisoned him where he received regular beatings for not wanting to be a Romanian. So our family had to leave the eastern part of Hungary. However, when my father would not join the socialist Nazi party and refused the order to leave Hungary and go to Germany, he became the target of the Nazi regime. The Nazi-controlled media accused him and called him a Jewish- and Russian-lover traitor.

Soon after, he was arrested, tried and sentenced to be hanged. Our family was slated for internment in a temporary holding camp until they could move us to one of the concentration or work camps. We were unbelievably fortunate this time as my father was freed by the people who came to witness the highly publicized hanging and the war ended soon after.

—⚬—

After WWII we were hoping for freedom and independence, but Soviet, Romanian, Serbian, Bulgarian, and Czech armies stayed. Under the pressure of the Soviet and allied occupying armies we were forced to accept the mutilation of our country, reducing the size to 29% of the original Hungarian Kingdom. We also lost millions of our people to neighboring newly created countries. A new socialist puppet government was put in place by Stalin.

My father worked tirelessly to help restore our remaining country after WWII devastation in a similar position he had held before the war. His work was appreciated by the people and even the new socialist governments until he refused to join the Communist Party. Then the usual game began. The socialist controlled media started the campaign to discredit my father, calling him a German lover and Jew hater dangerous man. Soon after, he had to report to the Secret Police HQ on a regular basis. Since they could not convert him, he was forced to retire.

My father was ready to start a new career when the Communist Party won the election in 1948 by cunningly taking over the most popular party with the most populous votes - the Smallholders - by imprisoning its leaders and later executing them. From this time on, they started to replace and eliminate the past leadership and their families.

We were slated for forced labor camp when my father died in 1949. But they didn't stop persecuting us, they took away our pensions, home, land, farm and kicked us out of schools. Maybe because my father passed away, they didn't send us to the labor camp.

We brothers and sisters had to earn some money to survive but we could only find jobs as hourly laborers. My mother's weaving and knitting helped put some food on the table but not enough for us to survive. We gradually traded all our furniture for food; the piano for a gallon of butter, the dressers for flour, the mirrors for salt, the couch for vegetables, the bedframes and nightstands for cooking oil or lard. - For seven years we couldn't afford to buy meat, butter or any sweets.

Without bed frames, we ended up sleeping on the floor or putting the bedsprings on bricks to be somewhat elevated. The three bedroom apartment for 7 of us was too expensive so we had to sublease one of the bedrooms, kitchen, and bathroom to pay for our part. However, we felt fortunate to be alive and to escape the real hardship in forced labor camps.

In 1950 the government permitted the opening of two private schools where we could be admitted but we had no money for tuition. After getting a job at the school and my mother offering our remaining Persian rugs for payments, we were accepted. The school was excellent, we had the best teachers and professors of my life. In fact, we enjoyed this school so much that during the winter times when the outside temperature dropped to minus 30 degrees or below and no coal was available to heat the classrooms, we still attended sitting in a winter jacket, gloves on and covered with blankets just to hear the professors' teachings. During national school competitions, we often achieved the top recognition in mathematics, foreign languages approved by the socialist government (learning or teaching English was punishable by long prison sentences), and sports.

We had a hard time finding even summer jobs as on all job applications we had to list the name and pre-1945 occupation of our parents and we already had been categorized as the undesirable class. In a socialist state only the factory workers and subsistence farmers had privileges besides the Communist party members, Secret Police, and high government officials. Therefore, to get even a temporary job I had to skip entering my father's name on the application, instead, I just put, "DECEASED" and left the occupation part blank. In most cases, I got away with the incomplete application and was able to get menial jobs. During the school year, I was able to earn some money by tutoring in the field of science and playing in orchestras. I was even able to get extra food based on good performances in athletics and swimming. The socialist state rewarded good performers in sports by supplementing their diet by providing high-energy foods, such as butter and natural sugars.

Possibly, we were the most fortunate family in the Communist Party-controlled socialist states. In spite of being classified as a family of undesirables, class "X", we survived with minimal punishment but just with a lot of hardships. Even the relatives had to stop all contact with us in order not to be labeled with the same classification and lose their jobs.

Most families, with similar backgrounds as ours, had more painful experiences, if they survived at all. The conditions in the work camps were deplorable, worse than the concentration camps. Based on what I know, only the Gulag camps were harder to survive. A good example of the way the socialist government worked is that all these undesirable families who were sent to work camps had to be there only for a few years according to the sentences given by the People's (kangaroo)[15] courts. However, there was no follow up, so once the family got there, they had to stay until they died or were too sick to work.

I know of instances where the treatment of some of the families were so evil and ensanguined that I don't have the stomach to describe them. The only survivor of these gruesome interrogations I know is Tibor Part. He suffered innumerable painful electric shock treatments in the prison for many years while his pregnant wife was put in a press until the unborn infant died. People who were tortured to death and didn't have families or relatives alive were ground up and dumped into the Danube river.

During the Communist Party control of our socialist government, the Secret Police or the Russian KGB took at least 800,000 people, mostly Christian males, not to be seen again. We only know that many of the people taken ended up in one of the GULAG camps in Russia.

CLOSE ENCOUNTERS WITH THE OPPOSITE SEX IN THE WORKPLACE

I had a good rapport with all my associates and employees. There was mutual trust, I'd like to think that I earned by being honest, fair and respectful toward everybody from the housekeeper to the president. Many of the employees often turned to me for advice

---

[15] Socialist state appointed judges from the Communist Party members (sometimes ex-criminals) without any background in Law and no defense lawyer was allowed.

in personal matters, told me things I really didn't want to know, and sometimes included some intimate topics.

My regular weekly brief visits in their offices, usually in the early morning, with each employee reporting to me directly or indirectly, and my open-door policy were most likely the reasons to have established such a good relationship, even when the department exceeded 120 employees. Of course, all employees had their own personality, some more reserved and some more outgoing.

I always had my private office and a small conference room which offered true privacy for anyone who wanted to share confidential information. Just about half of the people took advantage of this opportunity to share information or ask advice from me - they knew I listened, could be trusted, and really cared. However, there were some who preferred to talk to me about private matters outside the office environment and invited me for a drink, just for a chat and sometimes for dinner or lunch.

I was not always available at lunch time because of my regular exercise routine of running or swimming at least 2 times a week. A good workout was a big stress relief for me. On occasions, male colleagues joined me running on tracks at nearby school grounds or parks, but when I went swimming only females came along - I'm still not sure why.

This type of atmosphere was also conducive to teamwork and partnership building.

Everybody knew I cared, could be trusted and appreciated their quality work. This included my secretaries as my English spelling is still atrocious. My secretaries made me the top specification and business letter writer at just about every company I worked and of course, I gave them all the well-deserved credit, and they appreciated it. - Now that I have started writing again, I really miss my ex-secretaries.

In order to improve the ratio of female engineers, I went to the extra effort to find them. In those times few women graduated as engineers. Most of the young ladies preferred arts over sciences.

I was fortunate because I had my own cost-center and could pay the appropriate and fair salaries based on knowledge, abilities, productivity and experiences regardless of gender. We had more women to hire when they learned of our practices and policies. New employees often helped to find other engineers who were good, but typically underpaid. Many of the women engineers were reserved, serious, others were more outgoing and free-spirited.

My first close encounter with the opposite sex with whom I worked was in the mid-1960s. She was a nice looking young engineer from the East coast, seemingly reserved and always professionally dressed. I appreciated her hard work and mannerism. She often came by my office just to say hello or share some recent experiences she had after she moved to the West coast that were unique or funny for her. Food wise, she missed the Eastern style deep-dish pizza and couldn't find anything close to her favorite Lake Champagne.

She organized a private party for our small group of 12 engineers. The party was a big success, well planned and organized. There was good food and new entertaining games we could all participate in. Everybody enjoyed it and we had a lot of fun.

About a month later she came and told me she was planning another party and I would like to come? "Of course," was my answer depending on the time as I was going for a hike in the mountains the coming weekend. "That is OK as I planned it for the following weekend". "That's great," was my answer, "What can I bring?". "Just yourself", she responded.

On the party day, I put my suit on, selected a bright-colored necktie for the fun time and arrived about 15 minutes after the designated time. There were two surprises; I was the first one to arrive. She was not wearing her usual conservative formal outfit. She was casually dressed in just a short bright checkered skirt and a cream-colored blouse. I complained that she didn't tell me to dress casually but she smiled and asked me to take my jacket and tie off. She helped me to do both. We talked and I complained that nobody else showed up, so she smiled and said, "That's Ok, let's eat". She led me into her kitchen where a small table was set for two and a fine bottle of wine in the middle. When she opened the oven door a wonderful aroma filled the air that made my saliva run. I offered to open the wine bottle and she handed me the cork puller and smiled. We sat down to eat and it became more than obvious that this is a different party than I had imagined or expected.

Since I was unprepared for the unexpected situation and I had no emotional or sexual attraction to her, I behaved professionally, as a European gentleman. Surprisingly, she didn't feel awkward and we had a long and pleasant conversation on different subjects from classical music to formal dancing. We parted company pretty late that Saturday night and we never talked about this event ever again even though we had daily contacts in the office.

She didn't give up and tried again one more time about a month later, but I politely turned her down.

About 8 years later she came for an interview at my company in a different department. After the interview, she came to my office to see me. I barely recognized her, she was exceptionally attractive in her form-fitting light grey suit and a different hairdo, but her sweet smile was the same. She was so nice looking, pleasant with an enticing scent I wished I had the time to take her for lunch. In the few minutes we had she told me her life story summary. She got married, divorced and had a beautiful daughter but she was still interested in me as she thought I had great potential. By that time I was happily married to a wonderful and very smart young lady and we had three young boys. I was honest and told her, "If I were single, I would jump at the opportunity to really get to know you." She gave me her sweet smile, left and never saw her since.

I found out weeks later that she refused the very attractive offer given to her by the other department head.

After this unexpected meeting with her, I spent some time soul-searching to figure out why I didn't find her as attractive and sexy at the last party we had together.

—⁂—

The other young lady whom I found very attractive from the beginning, worked in the same department under a different manager. She was always very nice to me and even helped me on occasion to get express service from other departments as she was very popular and knew how to pull strings. I was unaware of any special treatment from her until my secretary called it to my attention. Believing that it was just a platonic relationship and she was a go-getter, I invited her for lunch to thank her for all the help I received from her. I was careful not to show my attraction to her.

I asked her to bring her husband along to one of the upcoming company picnics and treated her with the utmost respect.

She did bring her husband and I congratulated him on finding such a smart and beautiful wife. He was a pleasant looking gentleman in great physical shape, so I wondered as to why his wife would show so much attention to me. She continued to be very nice, helpful and often assisted me when my secretary was gone.

About three months later I received such an attractive offer from another company that I could not refuse. To my surprise, most of the engineers reporting to me before wanted to follow me, including her.

I did have to hire a few new engineers at the company so I was able to hire some of my ex-employees and eventually her as well. I felt safe despite my attraction to her as we were both married and very busy at the new company. She became a star performer and got things done expeditiously even across other departments while completing her assignments on time. She was able to set up private meetings for me with the busy CEO even though other department heads could not. I considered her one of my most productive, reliable and trusted employees. At her review time, I promoted her with a substantial raise. At breaks, she came to my office to chat and I welcomed her company as she had a very pleasant voice, she was well read, kept up with current events both in the office and outside, and always with a lovely smile. She also shared interesting events in her life, problems, possible solutions, vacation plans, difficulties both in technical and emotional areas. At some point, I both looked forward to and worried about her visits because of the strong physical and emotional attraction I felt for her.

One day she came to my office crying and shaking. Of course, I closed the door for privacy as I genuinely wanted to know what bothered her so much. It was the first time I saw her pale, shaking and crying. She was the first crying and shaking woman I had ever seen that was still attractive and beautiful in spite of her distressed state.

I embraced her and after a while with shaking warm lips and heavy tears she whispered in my left ear that Al, her husband, died in a climbing accident in South America. I could not help her in any other ways except for letting her talk and I would listen with understanding and compassion.

Someone knocked on my door and I had to let her out of my arms. I sat her down in the chair right next to my desk. When I opened the door my secretary was standing there and asking what happened as she saw her heading to my office crying.

I had to tell my secretary what happened with Al while she was still crying and shaking. I asked the secretary to keep it confidential until she is ready to announce it herself, hold all my calls and don't let anybody disturb us. Then, I asked my secretary to stay as I was afraid that I might hug her again, keep her close to me, which would be inappropriate and unfair to her. However, with crying eyes she stood up and came to me, looked at mine with her sad red eyes and put her arm around my neck. I could not resist, I pulled her close to me, embraced her.

My secretary stood there for a moment, turned around, walked out and closed the door behind her.

I eased up on my embrace, but she would not let me go for a long time. I wanted her to talk and I had to wait several minutes before she let me go and would sit down. She kept quiet for a while and when her tears stopped she started to talk. My heart went out for her as she spoke so softly still with those beautiful quivering red lips telling me how her life was from childhood to the present. She almost talked through the entire lunchtime and I listened with rapt attention. Just before 1 PM she stopped, looked up to me and smiled. I didn't understand, but she continued telling me that this is the first time somebody really paid attention and listened to what she had to say. She claimed that every other man beside Al and I didn't truly respected her and just wanted to have sex from her.

Her sweet smile always gave me happy and warm feelings and I wanted to hug her again, but I resisted.

I walked out of my office with her to lead her back to her desk and noticed my secretary still guarding my office. I thanked her and sent her out for lunch.

The place was practically empty, most of the engineers were out to lunch. When we got to her desk she asked me to hug her before she set down. I obliged reluctantly as I had warm and compassionate feelings for her especially during her very difficult and trying time. I told her to take some time off but she refused. Who else, she claimed, will listen to and understand me as I?

When I walked back to the office my secretary just returned from lunch and thanked me for the way I handled the situation, saying, "You're a good boss, everybody else would have been afraid to hug her and that was what she needed".

She came to work every working day but often had to take time off to handle all the official business associated with her husband's death. It took her a long time to come to terms with her loss but her sweet smiles returned about three months later. When she started smiling again I realized how much I missed them. The next morning, I went to her desk and thanked her for the smile and told her I was happy to see her getting back to normal. While talking I leaned on her desk looking in her eyes and she put her hand on mine. She smiled and said, "We need to talk at your convenience after work, or can we meet at a nice place to have a drink?" Feeling her gentle touch on my hand gave me a real tingly feeling and I couldn't resist her invitation. Instead of waiting, she suggested going out for lunch by the airport where she knows a nice place to talk. I agreed.

We took her small sports car instead of my sedan and she drove us to this hole-in-the-wall place hidden between two large elm trees. The inside was surprisingly spacious and we were escorted to a nice private cubicle far in the back. She had obviously made a reservation. From this point on I remember everything that happened and was said.

She had a bloody-mary and I had a martini with olives, she ordered a Caesar salad and I a BLT sandwich. I asked her how she was coping with her loss, what her plans were for the future, what her wishes and wants were. She was smiling all the time while telling me all her wishes and desires, which included a vacation in Europe, getting a master's degree, possibly changing jobs, visiting the opera more often, playing more on the piano and singing in the shower.

We started to eat when she asked me similar questions. I started in the second half of my sandwich when she reached across the table and grabbed my left hand and started her monolog saying:

there were only two men in her life that really respected her, but she really only loved one of them and it's I! I knew she liked me and so did I liked her but initially I didn't know how to respond to the word; "love".

After a long pause, I responded that I cannot divorce my loving wife and leave my wonderful smart sons and I think our infatuation with each other is a temporary thing at best. She held my hand even stronger and claimed that she was not asking me to divorce my wife and leave my family, she just wanted to be loved by me. She described many ways we could keep our relations secret both in the office and in our families. Her offer was so attractive and tempting after she described some of the details and plans to be together in intimate ways that I almost succumbed to the temptations. I remembered asking what happens if she got pregnant? Her eyes lit up and said, "That is what I want", but she soon added her ready and well-thought out plans to keep it secret and me out of the possible repercussions both at home and the office. My final words were that I could not ignore any son or daughter of mine and leave either one without a father.

When we finally concluded our conversations without finishing our meals, she took my "no-way" and my firm expressed reservations very negatively. I never saw any ladies with sader eyes and showing deeper disappointment. It seems like she worked out all the details on how to have an intimate relationship with me except she wasn't prepared for my negative response.

In retrospect, I don't know where my strength came from to reject such an attractive offer, but I think somebody up there watched out for me and her.

I went to work for a new start-up company, where all the long hours and hard work would make me forget her, but it didn't work! She tried to follow me, but I had the decency not to give her a job. However, I slowly and surely came to the realization that I'm more than capable of loving more than one woman at a time, but I'm happy we didn't complicate each other's and potentially many other's lives.

I have not kept in touch, but I heard that she wouldn't date anyone else for years. I'm sorry I was the cause of so much pain for her. I had lost all the contacts and have no idea about what happened to her, but I hope it turned out well for her.

ADDENDUM

DISCOVER YOUR TALENTS

BE THE ARCHITECT OF YOUR OWN LIFE

KELE D. GABOR

INTRODUCTION

For parents, teachers, mentors, friends and young adults who are interested in making their own or others' life better and more fulfilling.

This booklet is on how to find your *talents* and help you to discover what should be the *purpose* of your life.

Many failures are blamed on others, there are too many school dropouts, too much self-pity, too many people feel victimized, too many suicides, too many ruined lives, too many lost souls, and too many unfulfilled lives.

These difficulties listed above could be avoided or overcome by actively and honestly examining oneself and seeking solutions for the real problems of not knowing what should be the purpose of your life.

In this booklet the short exercises listed, if done with due diligence, will even help pessimists, people with depression, or low self-esteem to find their way out of their predicament.

"All of us are born for a reason, but all of us don't discover why."
- Danny Thomas

Be proactive in improving yourself, find your talents, your special abilities and develop them to become the architect of your own life!

WHAT THIS BOOKLET IS ABOUT

We are all born with a set of special talents, abilities, defined at conception by our unique DNA received from both our mother and father. Therefore, it is the primary responsibility of our parents, then teachers, mentors, professors, friends and oneself to discover, develop, and improve these gifts and put them to good use.

Parents; children are our future, plant love in their hearts and shower them with wisdom, life's lessons, guide them to find and develop their talents and abilities.

Talents and abilities are gifts but good character has to be built through courage and determination!

Our environment, as created or made for us, will help develop, improve and sometimes hide, diminish or even destroy these talents or abilities. Under the right circumstances even serious disabilities could be overcome! Examples are many: people born without arms can develop uncanny abilities using their legs, feet and toes to compensate for the missing extremities; individuals born without eyesight often can perform tasks that able-bodied people cannot. However, even under ideal environments and optimum circumstances all of one's talents, special abilities and ingenuity will be very difficult to identify. Therefore, it is a lifelong process to find most of those gifts!

The road to self-fulfillment is finding one's talents and abilities, tasks you do well, and things that satisfy you. Then create a path to put most of your talents and interests to work. The instructions in this booklet will guide you to find a place in life where you can be more content and productive in what you're doing and help our youth who are not sure what career to choose after graduating from High School.

Each one of us born on this Earth is here to learn, love, hope, appreciate and share with others most of the talents one has. True self-fulfillment and happiness comes from finding our abilities, developing them and using them for the benefit of others!

When you love what you do, the result will be a happier life. Your happiness with a positive outlook on life will be sensed by people around you and it will be contagious leaving a good impression and feelings about you.

"Search for yourself, by yourself. Do not allow others to make your path for you. It is a road, and yours alone. Others may walk with you, but no-one can walk it for you."

- American Native Code of Ethics

HOW TO START

L et's suppose you're sixteen years old, or a senior in High School, or just unhappy with your current job and want to know what fields you should pursue to find more enjoyment in your life. To achieve these positive changes in your life follow the instructions in the *Steps* below which must be done in *sequence*.

Step 1.

Get a sheet of paper (8x11") and fold it in half *lengthwise* and *number* each page from 1 to 4.

Please keep in mind that these steps must be done privately and your work should be treated as a confidential diary.

Only on *Page 3* where you can ask others, like teachers, parents and friends to point out some of the talents you might not be aware of.

Step 2.

Page 1. "What I like to do" Start listing all activities which you like or enjoy doing and if you cannot fill up this page, include things you think you would very much like to do and most likely enjoy doing.

Two examples (A & B): "What I like to do":

A	B
Read Books	Art & Design
Play Soccer	Help Others
Solve Math Problems	Water Skiing
Baseball & Tennis	Solving Problems
Swimming	Fishing
Listen to Music	Come up with new Ideas
Photography	Being practical
Walk and Hike	Sing
Play Chess	Computer Games
Date Girls	Dance
Find Minerals	Go to Parties
Trek Wild Animals	Draw and Paint
Hunt	Shop Online
Play Bridge	Watch TV

Step 3.

Page 2. "What I think I'm good at" Start listing activities you think you're good at.

Examples:	A	B
	Mathematics	Water Skiing
	Sciences	Fishing
	Gymnastics	Camping
	Track & Field	Cooking and Baking
	Dancing	Painting
	Archery	Arts and Crafts
	Swimming	Caring for Animals
	Tutoring	Organizing
	Team Sports	Planning Parties

Please note what you think you're good at is usually a subset of what you like to do, and which one knows instinctively.

Step 4.

Page 3. "List of awards, recognitions and praises I received for my accomplishments".

Here you list any activities, papers, compliments, awards, or "job well done" from your teachers, parents, coaches or others.

Example:

> Top of the class in Sciences
>
> Dedicated Team Player
>
> Recognition for Mentoring
>
> Medals in Track & Field
>
> Good in Mathematics
>
> Good Book Reports
>
> Music Award in playing the Flute
>
> Good in Drawing

This part of the exercise will certify and validate many of your talents by the fact that they were recognized by others, and sometimes even add to your list of abilities.

This is the only step where asking others for help as teachers, parents, friends, mentors or others are permitted and recommended as you might have forgotten or be unaware of some of the talents you might have.

Again, this list may be a subset of what you think you are good at with possible surprise additions you find out from consulting others.

Step 5.

Once you complete your first *3 pages* you should go back to review and determine where your real talents and abilities are. It is essential at this stage to understand your talents, good traits and capabilities, and be aware of what kind of things you like to do. This will help you to select activities to improve your skills, knowledge and profession to pursue and to ensure success in your selected fields of endeavors.

HOW TO COMPLETE THIS EXERCISE

Step 6.

At this point you should have a pretty good understanding of your talents, skills and abilities to complete the final *Page 4* which will help you find your calling and to pick a profession or new fields for yourself.

Page 4 will have three parts (A,B,C) and you have to answer all in sequence in order to write a good *Vision* statement for yourself at the conclusion of this exercise.

Step 7.

Page 4A, "What are my weaknesses or shortcomings?"

Please note: People who don't know their weaknesses cannot really succeed in life, and cannot be truly self-confident. Lack of understanding in this area can lead to a lot of frustration and a less productive life. Also keep in mind that some strengths can beget weaknesses. Examples: typically perfectionists are unaware of many possible shortcomings; they like to do everything by themselves, therefore they cannot delegate, are inefficient time managers, not good team players, and weak leaders.

Knowing your weaknesses will give you more self confidence, be more realistic of what you can or cannot do, and of course be more productive by concentrating on activities you are good at. Weaknesses or shortcomings do *not* reduce your worth unless one chooses to hide or ignore them. Nobody is perfect!

A few examples are listed below to prove the above points:

- Let's suppose you want to start a business and if you do *not* know your shortcomings, how do you know what kind of partner or help to pick or hire to compensate for your weaknesses?
- Finding the right partner for life requires you to know where you need help to ensure a good, balanced, successful, and harmonious marriage where weaknesses are compensated by one another.
- While many people are multifaceted, knowing both their strengths and weaknesses will be critical in selecting or putting together productive teams, will help family unity, companies, or any organization.

Step 8.

Page 4B, "If you were the devil how would I tempt myself?"

This is a very important step, whether you believe in the devil or not, to know what kind of things you *must avoid at all costs* in order to be able to follow your Vision and ensure a good deal of satisfaction and success in life.

I know or witnessed what might happen if one ignores this step:

- A successful professional and happy family man ruined his life as he never listed, and wanted to hide, his "addiction to gambling".
- A high-ranking career officer after 10 years of service ruined his family life as he missed admitting to "sex addiction".
- Alcoholism, drug addiction, and any other bad habits can lead to unwanted failures and must be identified for knowing what to *avoid at any cost.*

Step 9, "My VISION Statement" - the final and very important step!

This is the most important step to complete and finalize this exercise, as it will define the path for you to take to a more fulfilling and satisfying earthly life. This part also typically takes the longest time to hone and refine. While doing Steps 1 through 8 could be done in a few days, but for many people a good Vision statement may take weeks or months to perfect. Of course, it should be revisited and improved as needed. Reviewing and revising your Vision Statement on your Birthdays could benefit you in many ways.

Page 4C, "What is my VISION Statement?"

After completing all the previous steps one can start listing professions, work, activities on a separate sheet of paper, which would optimize the use of one's talents and come to conclusions about what field or fields will best make use of most of one's talents, skills, and abilities. *At the end it must be narrowed down to a short simple sentence.*

There are many books written and lectures given on the importance of having a positive Vision Statement. Successful businesses, ventures, organizations, teams and individuals use their Vision statement effectively to guide them to success.

Many examples of Vision Statements can be found in company brochures as Mission Statements. You could also ask happy and successful people to share their vision with you.

The important feature of the Vision Statement, besides being a positive single sentence, is that it has to be *open-ended*. If it is not open-ended, it becomes a goal instead of a *guiding principle* for the rest of your life. Goals are always temporary as when achieved, your efforts are completed. Vision statements with possible minot changes should last your lifetime and maybe beyond as other people might follow in your footsteps.

One good example of a Vision statement is TOYOTA's which made them the Number One auto manufacturer in the world:

"We build the best and the most cars."

Note: Their Vision Statement is open-ended as one can always improve the quality and increase the number of cars manufactured. It also attracts proud engineers and workers who want to excel and want to design and build high quality cars. It also draws potential buyers looking for high quality and reliability!"

My teachers also had beautiful Vision Statements:

- In Elementary school - *"Instill the desire to learn in every one of my pupils."*

- In High School - *"Find the talents, abilities and help develop them for each of my students."*
- In Junior College - (Use a three pronged approach in character development.) - *"Improve spiritual, physical and intellectual quality in each of my students."*

Once you complete all nine steps for your own satisfaction, review them yearly as you might find additional talents or develop new skills which could be put to good use!

- After finishing, most rational people will come to the realization that each one of us is here on earth for a reason or *purpose.*
- *What is the purpose of your life?*

To find out what your *"purpose of life"* should be, complete the described steps in this booklet as no one else is in charge of your happiness but you!

HELPFUL INFORMATION

Many people will have occasion to introduce themselves, either before, during or right after an interview where knowing your *Vision* will give you a definite edge!

Just imagine you're in an elevator with the president of a company for whom you want to work. You'll typically have only a minute to impress him or her and you must be ready to introduce, and sell yourself and your talents. There are key elements you need to know and prepare for when such a golden opportunity presents itself.

Initially, you have to be able to start a conversation which can only be accomplished if you can say something impressive about the company, the product or leadership. This step should suffice to get the individual's attention so you can introduce yourself.

Self-introduction has four key elements to impress:

- Who you are,
- Your Vision, (may be paraphrased to suit the job you want to have)
- What you want to do and
- Why.? (The "why" always has to contain a positive and catchy phrase which benefits the company, customers or the community.)

Make a point to find something beautiful everyday in your life.

When you meet people, smile.

Find good in every person you meet.

Make a point of learning something new every day.

Happiness comes from serving others.

Nobody who helps others is useless.

There is no way to erase a useful life.

A useful life is one which lives beyond you.

Choose the difficult *right* rather than the easy *wrong*.

Cannot change the past but can influence the future.

You are in charge of your Happiness.

Happiness can be enhanced by others but it doesn't depend on others.

Everybody needs to be loved, but also to love self as well.

Love is the only thing that can be divided without being diminished.

When it comes to going after what you love, don't take no for an answer.

- Regina Brett

A blind person asked St. Anthony: "Can there be anything worse than losing your eyesight?" He replied. "Yes, losing your Vision!"

- For those who know some Latin, Roman culture, and appreciate word matrix:

R	O	T	A	S
O	P	E	R	A
T	E	N	E	T
A	R	E	P	O
S	A	T	O	R

CPSIA information can be obtained
at www.ICGtesting.com
Printed in the USA
BVHW031230270721
612866BV00022B/175